ARGUMENT
IN THE REAL WORLD

Teaching
Adolescents to
Read and Write
Digital Texts

ARGUMENT in the REAL WORLD

Kristen Hawley Turner | Troy Hicks

HEINEMANN
Portsmouth, NH

Heinemann
361 Hanover Street
Portsmouth, NH 03801–3912
www.heinemann.com
Offices and agents throughout the world

"Dedicated to Teachers" is a trademark of Greenwood Publishing Group, Inc.

The authors and publisher wish to thank those who have generously given permission to reprint borrowed material:

Figure 1.1: Photograph and text excerpt by Jennifer Raff from "Dear parents, you are being lied to," posted March 25, 2014, to her blog *Violent Metaphors*: http://violentmetaphors.com. Used by permission of the author.

Table 1.1: Inquiry Square of Declarative and Procedural Knowledge of Form and Substance adapted from *Oh, Yeah?! Putting Argument to Work Both in School and Out* by Michael W. Smith, Jeffrey D. Wilhelm, and James E. Fredricksen. Copyright © 2012 by Michael W. Smith, Jeffrey D. Wilhelm, and James E. Fredricksen. Published by Heinemann, Portsmouth, NH. All rights reserved.

(credits continue on page vi)

Cataloging-in-Publication Data is on file at the Library of Congress.

ISBN: 978-0-325-08675-0

Editor: Tobey Antao
Production editor: Patty Adams
Cover and interior designs: Suzanne Heiser
Typesetter: Shawn Girsberger
Manufacturing: Steve Bernier

Printed in the United States of America on acid-free paper
20   19   18   17   16   VP   1   2   3   4   5

(continued from page iv)

Contents

Acknowledgments

We started this book with the understanding that we were entering uncharted territory in thinking about how to teach argument writing in digital spaces, at least in comparison to the ways that argument writing traditionally gets taught in elementary, middle, and high school classrooms.

As with all good scholarship, our work builds on the writing of others who have articulated both the thinking and the teaching of written argument. Most notably, we acknowledge George Hillocks Jr. (1934–2014), whose scholarship and mentorship influenced us heavily. George passed away as we were drafting the proposal for this book and we did not have the opportunity to talk through our ideas with him, but we remember him in these pages.

We also are indebted to the teachers who contributed to our thinking through casual conversations, workshop sessions, and online interactions—there were many of you, too many to count or acknowledge properly without leaving someone out. We do, however, want to offer special appreciation to those who met with us, talked with us, and shared both their students' work and their practice with us: Janelle Bence, Sheila Cooperman, Alex Corbitt, Laura Garrison, Sara Kajder, Lauren King, Allison Marchetti, Valerie Mattessich, Dawn Reed, and Betsy Reid. Your ideas and student work greatly shaped the argument we wanted to make. Troy would also like to extend appreciation to his writing group—Jim Fredricksen, Anne Whitney, and Leah Zuidema—for their feedback.

Jennifer Stewart, a graduate student in the Fordham Graduate School of Education, helped with so many aspects of writing that we cannot list them all here. Likewise, the team at Heinemann—including Amanda Bondi, Sarah Fournier, Kim Cahill, Lisa Fowler, Patty Adams, Suzanne Heiser, and Steve Bernier—helped us navigate permissions (not an easy task for this book) and supported us during a long journey.

Another member of that team, Tobey Antao, was a clear, consistent, and—when appropriate—critical voice in our work on this book. She coached; she questioned; she pushed; and, most important, she argued. In so doing, she helped us create a book that we feel is important, timely, and accessible. Thank you, Tobey, for all you have done during this project.

Finally, we thank our families for understanding the long, stressful hours of writing to deadlines. Without their support, this work would not have been possible.

A Tool for You: The Companion Wiki

It is always a challenge to write about digital tools and texts in a printed book. We know—as readers ourselves—that sometimes it is best to click on a link and *see* what the writers have described.

   Thus, the companion wiki for this book provides all of the links, chapter by chapter, so that you can easily access them. You will also find resources—some from this book and some curated by us as well as other teachers in our networks—to support you as you implement instruction in digital arguments.

   Finally, in the spirit of digital reading and writing, we hope that you will contribute ideas to the wiki so that we and others can learn from your experiences.

Follow the QR code above, or visit http://argumentintherealworld.wikispaces.com/.

CHAPTER 1

THE NATURE OF ARGUMENT IN A DIGITAL WORLD

Nearly every time we open an inbox, turn on a TV or radio, check a social network, or even engage in casual conversation about current events, we are presented with arguments. Like us, our students, who are beginning to use tablets and smartphones at increasingly younger ages, are exposed to a variety of arguments. Some of these arguments come from reliable sources that include credentialed experts and reputable news organizations. Others come from anonymous marketers and opinionated individuals who write blogs and discussion posts. All of us must make sense of the barrage of information.

Kristen recently received an example of one such argument in a status update from a friend who included a link to an article about children's vaccines. Figure 1.1 shows the title of that article with its accompanying image.

Kristen received this article in a stream of information, but the title and image immedi-

Dear parents, you are being lied to.

April 9, 2014 | by Anonymous

© Jennifer Raff. Used with permission.

Figure 1.1 Cover Image and Text from "Dear Parents, You Are Being Lied To"

ately captured her attention. She noticed that the article was "by Anonymous" and she began to think carefully about her reading. Who shared this with me? Do I trust that friend? Do I imagine that she perceives this article to contain factual and useful information? Then Kristen clicked on the link. Once there she began to notice a few other features of this text:

- The website is titled IFL Science, and yet there is no "About Us" link on the site. A quick link to Facebook reveals the site is called "I F***king Love Science," a site that, upon further investigation, includes "meme-style science illustrations," "plain-speaking summaries of the latest research," and "links to oddities" (Teeman 2013).

- A note appears in bold print at the top of the post: "The content of this article was written by Dr. Jennifer Raff for her blog, *Violent Metaphors*. It is being rehosted here with permission. You can click on the above hyperlink to view the original and engage in the lively discussion in the comments section." The blog title is indeed a link to http://violentmetaphors .com, a blog with the tagline "Thoughts from the intersection of science, pseudoscience, and conflict."

- Dr. Raff's blog does have an "About Me" page, with this information as part of her introduction: "I study the genomes of modern and ancient peoples in order to uncover details of human prehistory. You can learn more about my scientific publications and credentials here and here." The words *here* and *here* link to her curriculum vitae and her profile on Academia.edu, respectively.

With just thirty seconds of investigation, Kristen determined that—despite the potentially off-putting name of the host website, IFL Science (which certainly wouldn't make it past many school Internet filters)—the original blog post comes from a credentialed doctor and that IFL was created by a PhD student in biology, Elise Andrew (Teeman 2013). Considering her own perspective as a researcher and parent, and understanding a bit about the controversies related to childhood vaccinations, Kristen determined Raff would be a credible author, and she continued to read on. We acknowledge that Kristen may have put a little more effort into making this determination than most readers, especially teenage readers.

Let's examine Dr. Raff's argument as Kristen, or any reader, might have engaged with it.

> *In light of <u>recent outbreaks</u> of measles and other vaccine preventable illnesses, and the refusal of anti-vaccination advocates to acknowledge the problem, I thought it was past time for this post.*
>
> Dear parents,
> <u>You are being lied to</u>. The people who claim to be acting in the best interests of your children are putting their health and even lives <u>at risk</u>.
>
> They say that measles isn't a deadly disease.
> But <u>it is</u>.
>
> They say that chickenpox isn't that big of a deal.
> But <u>it can be</u>.
>
> They say that the flu isn't dangerous.
> But <u>it is</u>.
>
> They say that whooping cough isn't so bad for kids to get.
> But <u>it is</u>.
>
> They say that vaccines aren't that effective at preventing disease.
> But 3 million children's lives <u>are saved every year by vaccination</u>, and 2 million <u>die every year from vaccine-preventable illnesses</u>.
>
> They say that "natural infection" is better than vaccination.
> But <u>they're wrong</u>.
>
> They say that vaccines haven't been rigorously tested for safety.
> But vaccines <u>are subjected to a higher level of scrutiny than any other medicine</u>. For example, <u>this study</u> tested the safety and effectiveness of the pneumococcal vaccine in more than 37,868 children.

Even in these first few lines, Dr. Raff has begun using of variety of moves to assert her position that parents are being lied to about giving children vaccines.

Her first link leads to the About.com health page related to statistics about current measles outbreaks. Her second link, "You are being lied to," leads to an article on Forbes.com about one doctor who has made an effort to tell parents that vaccinations do more harm than good. The links continue, with connections to the World Health Organization, the Centers for Disease Control, and the National Institutes of Health, among others. Each one of the points where she articulates the effects of the disease through "it is" or "it can be" links to a scientific study shared by one of these organizations. The article continues with more than sixty hyperlinks to other resources selected by Dr. Raff to accentuate her argument that vaccination is, indeed, a worthwhile and generally safe procedure for all children.

Finally, Kristen looked closely at something seemingly obvious—the structure of the text. Quite literally, she examined the way the words were put together into sentences, paragraphs, and an entire essay—all meant for the screen. If the author had tried to refute a claim with only the words "But they're wrong" in a print essay, the argument would have looked look flimsy and unsubstantiated. Even adding a list of parenthetical citations behind each statement of "But they're wrong" would likely not have had the same effect as clicking on a link to a reputable source such as the WHO or CDC.

However, because the author was consciously crafting a piece of digital writing, she wrote the essay with the links in mind as essential support for her argument, not just hypertext add-ons. Conversely, Kristen observed that if the piece had been written more like a print argument, in which each point was exhaustively explained, including numerous links might have seemed superfluous (or even unnecessarily distracting). In that sense, had this essay been written to the standards of citation for MLA or APA style, the natural rhythm of Dr. Raff's voice would have been broken by citations. Given that, Kristen wondered: Would she—or other readers—have read the article if, at first glance, it had looked daunting or lengthy?

In short, Kristen noticed how Dr. Raff used links as evidence to support her claims. She was curious about the extended conversation—and debate—that the digital text invited. She considered whether sharing it with her network would, in effect, be seen as making a claim itself. All of these moves required careful thought about the nature of the argument being made in this digital text, for it is precisely the digital component that opens up a whole new world of argumentation.

What Is Argument in a Digital World?

As Kristen's experience with this blog post shows, we read arguments every day. We are inundated by information—and opinions and misinformation—on our devices, and our students face the same challenges. For instance, Natalie, a ninth grader who has over seven hundred friends on Facebook, considers her digital reading "addicting." She spends time reading through the headlines of the news stories that appear on her AOL homepage when she opens her Internet browser, and she digs into articles that seem interesting. According to Natalie, she habitually reads the news before heading to Facebook, where she reads status updates and clicks through links that "look kind of interesting." But Natalie admits that, "sometimes when I'm reading stuff, if I see links, I'll keep clicking them, and I kind of get lost reading all of them because there's just so many to read."

Natalie is not alone in feeling overwhelmed by the information that she encounters. Like all of us, she needs to sort through a variety of texts and make sense of each within the network where it exists. Status updates. Hashtags. Blogs. Infographics. Web searches. Any text that we encounter—fiction or nonfiction, print or digital—is at some level presenting us with an argument. Lunsford, Ruszkiewicz, and Walters (2013) begin the sixth edition of their popular textbook, *Everything's an Argument,* with the following reflection:

> [A]nyone, anywhere, with access to a smart phone, can mount an argument
> that can circle the globe in seconds . . . The clothes you wear, the foods you
> eat, and the groups you decide to join make nuanced, sometimes unspoken
> arguments about who you are and what you value. So an argument can be any
> text—written, spoken, aural or visual—that expresses a point of view. (p. 5)

All of the points that these authors make are as true now as they have been for decades, if not centuries. That said, digital media add new layers to written arguments:

- Readers and writers can now be in conversation with each other regularly.

- We can counter arguments immediately, and those counterarguments can take the form of 140 characters, a comment in the textbox at the bottom of an article, or an entirely new blog post.

- We can put texts directly in conversation with each other, quite literally connecting one digital piece to another through links, making our embedded reasoning more (or potentially less) visible.

- We can create a visual argument in combination with—or in lieu of—a written argument.

- Everyone can and does make public arguments, and those arguments can reach far beyond an intended audience.

> Crafting arguments in a digital world could be one
> of our greatest opportunities to improve dialogue
> across cultures and continents, or it could contribute
> to creating or continuing bitter divides.

If we want our students, like Natalie, to be writing and analyzing real-world arguments—the kinds of digital texts that influence what they buy, whom they vote for, and what they believe about themselves and their world—we must teach them to understand both the logic of argument as well as how those arguments work when they are streaming in through a Twitter feed, a Facebook wall, viral videos, Internet memes, and links to other blogs or websites. A digital writer's ability to use data works differently in hyperlinked, multimodal contexts. What counts as evidence? How do we make connections from evidence to claims—as both readers and writers? And how do we change the way we structure arguments when our conversational partners can respond, in writing, almost immediately to our assertions? Crafting arguments in a digital world could be one of our greatest opportunities to improve dialogue across cultures and continents, or it could contribute to creating or continuing bitter divides.

And while we may still be concerned with the origins and intent of the Common Core State Standards, we can't deny the centrality of "argument" to those standards. Teaching students how to craft argumentative writing, including digital arguments, involves a process of reasoning, critical thinking, and problem solving—all skills that we need to use when participating in civic discourse.

A Brief Overview of Argument (or, What Makes a Strong Argument, Anyway?)

Formal logic, illustrated by Aristotle through *syllogisms*, follows a formulaic pattern:

Major Premise: All men are mortal.

Minor Premise: Socrates is a man.

Conclusion: Therefore, Socrates is mortal.

In *The Uses of Argument* (1958/2003), philosopher and educator Stephen Toulmin dissects syllogistic arguments and concludes, "Most of the arguments we have practical occasion to make use of are, one need hardly say, not of this type" (p. 124). Instead, Toulmin suggests a model for argument that focuses on practical uses and accounts for the complexity of human conversation, where arguments can be nested within each other and challenged at multiple levels—a description that applies to online discourse and digital writing as well. In fact, Toulmin explains that, in real-life situations, people make claims, and a conversational partner may challenge a claim by asking, "What have you got to go on?" (p. 13). This question requires the presentation of what Toulmin calls *data* and what the Common Core terms *evidence*. Once evidence has been presented, the conversational partner may ask, "How do you get there? (Toulmin, p. 98), or even more colloquially, "So what?" (Smith and Wilhelm 2006, p. 130). These types of prompts require a justification of the data that links it directly to the claim, or what Toulmin calls a *warrant*.

While the Common Core has ensured that *claim* and *evidence* are terms with which we are well acquainted, warrants are not as widely discussed and may fall under the umbrella of "reasoning." Warrants are amorphous, often implicit, and the hardest aspect of the Toulmin model to teach. However, they hold the key to why some well-crafted arguments fail to win over some audiences. Warrants are general statements that "act as bridges" (Toulmin, p. 98), explaining to the audience why a specific piece of evidence helps to prove the claim.

For example, you might claim that a high school day should not start before 8:30 a.m. and cite evidence showing that adolescents' sleep patterns make them less alert at 7:00 or 7:30, the time that most high school days typically begin. In this case, your warrant might be that schools have a responsibility to optimize learning and achievement by addressing students' biological needs.

"What?!?" your interlocutor might exclaim. "Making kids get up early teaches them responsibility!"

> If we consider that our students are now communicating to a global audience, the need for crafting successful arguments is more important than ever, and making implicit (or explicit) connections between evidence and claims is a key skill in this craft.

In this instance, the person to whom you are speaking does not believe that students' biological needs should be taken into account when determining school start times (or simply feels that the socioemotional habit of responsibility is more important), so your warrant requires backing—additional evidence or an entirely new argument. When a writer mistakenly assumes that an audience understands or accepts a warrant, the audience may be perplexed, if not enraged, and the writer may not understand why the argument was not successful. If we consider that our students are now communicating to a global audience, the need for crafting successful arguments is more important than ever, and making implicit (or explicit) connections between evidence and claims is a key skill in this craft.

The What and How of Writing: Declarative and Procedural Knowledge

Teacher, professor, and writing researcher George Hillocks Jr. suggests that traditional writing instruction—the kind that we see when teachers use the five-paragraph essay—focuses only on declarative knowledge, or *telling* students what a given genre should look like or include (and having them retell it in the form of a homework assignment, quiz, or test). Declarative knowledge, however, is not enough for an average writer to become great. In other words, just learning about the ways that writing works does not a good writer make. Hillocks contends that "the important knowledge is procedural" (1995, p. 99), or knowing how to produce the writing itself. Hillocks described the difference in this way:

> It is one thing to identify the characteristics of a piece of writing but quite another to produce an example of the type. . . . Knowledge of discourse, then, appears to have two dimensions: declarative knowledge, which enables identification of characteristics, and procedural knowledge, which enables production. (p. 121)

Thus, for any kind of writing, writers must have an understanding of the features of a particular genre, as well as the ability to compose an effective text. They must know what good writing is, and be able to produce good writing themselves. Smith, Wilhelm, and Fredricksen (2012) conceptualized this knowledge in a 4x4 grid that they call an "inquiry square" (p. 21). We have filled in their square with short descriptions in Table 1.1.

Table 1.1 Inquiry Square of Declarative and Procedural Knowledge of Form and Substance

	Form	Substance
Declarative Knowledge (Answers the question "what?"; easily tested)	What the writing itself is, including the generic/conventional characteristics	The content, topic, or subject of the writing
Procedural Knowledge (Answers the question "how?"; must be produced)	How to generate the needed characteristics	How to generate the content (inquiry)

Declarative and Procedural Knowledge in Digital Writing

It is one thing to produce an academic essay with word processing software while simultaneously accessing the Internet; a writer can draft, edit, and revise, all the while finding statistics or other evidence to support an idea. It is quite a distinct process to use the technology for a different purpose, such as to produce a blog post that requires links to other content and images that will catch the reader's attention while also contributing to the overall meaning of the post. Bud Hunt (2010), edublogger and technology integration coach, describes it this way: "Digital texts have the potential to make a big, juicy mess of a linear experience. Or to turn a so-so piece of writing into a masterful collection of references, linktributions, and pointers to other good stuff."

> ## Digital writing requires us to make intentional choices about what we want to say, as well as how we choose the media in which we say it.

Hunt's point that digital writers can make a "big, juicy mess" means that we have newfound opportunities to create rich, compelling arguments. However, without both the technical *and* the rhetorical knowledge to produce digital texts, writers may make just a mess. Thus, inserting a link is not just a technical activity; it is also a rhetorical activity that crosses knowledge of content and form. Numerous scholars in the field of rhetoric and composition, especially in the past decade, have demonstrated that digital writing demands both technical know-how and a deep understanding of audience, purpose, and context. Digital writing requires us to make intentional choices about what we want to say, as well as how we choose the media in which we say it (see, e.g., National Writing Project et al. 2010; Selber 2004; Selfe and Hawisher 2004; Writing in Digital Environments Research Center Collective 2005).

The considerations of declarative and procedural knowledge of both substance and form hold true for digital writing, but digital writing adds a layer of complexity. Digital media afford writers the opportunities to make hyperlinks, to embed images and videos, and to use space, formatting, and color to enhance their writing (Hicks 2013). In these modes, the tools of technology support a writer's rhetorical decisions. Because technology allows a writer more choices than just words on paper do, students need technological knowledge to be sophisticated digital writers. Knowledge of technology—by which we mean the hardware, software, and networks that a writer can use to produce a text—connects to both declarative and procedural knowledge as well as to the form and substance of the writing itself.

This technological knowledge is intimately connected to all four quadrants in Smith et al.'s grid, and, in fact, will deepen both declarative and procedural knowledge of form and substance. To illustrate that deepened perspective, Figure 1.2 represents our inquiry cube: the knowledge that digital writers need.

So what does this inquiry cube mean for teaching our students about digital writing? Let's look at a blog as an example. Miller and Shepherd (2004) describe blogs in this way:

> Blogs can be both public and intensely personal in possibly contradictory ways. They are addressed to everyone and at the same time to no one. They seem to serve no immediate practical purpose, yet increasing numbers of both writers and readers are devoting increasing amounts of time to them. The blog is a new rhetorical opportunity, made possible by technology that is becoming more available and easier to use, but it was adopted so quickly and widely that it must be serving well established rhetorical needs.

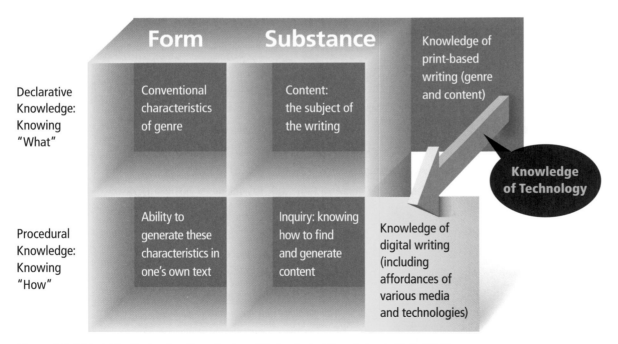

Figure 1.2 A Model for Declarative, Procedural, and Technological Knowledge in Digital Writing

Adapted from Hicks, T., K. H. Turner, and J. Stratton. 2013. "Reimagining a Writer's Process Through Digital Storytelling." *LEARNing Landscapes* 6 (2): 167–183.

We might use this description of blogs to introduce the features of a single blog post as a particular mode, or genre, of writing. In fact, in Chapter 3 we will delve more deeply into the declarative and procedural knowledge that a digital writer must have in order to craft an effective argument with a blog post. For the moment, we want to clearly state our overarching claim for this book: crafting digital arguments is similar to crafting traditional, text-based arguments in the sense that we rely on claims, evidence, and warrants to accomplish the goal; yet the process is different enough that we, as teachers, must explicitly teach both the modes of digital argument and the various media available to create digital arguments.

As Troy suggests in *Crafting Digital Writing*, "Craft is one piece of a larger genre puzzle" (Hicks 2013, p. 15). As students think through arguments with words, they also need to think "like artists, designers, recording engineers, photographers, and filmmakers" (p. 19) to take advantage of the elements of media—words, images, sounds, videos, and links—that contribute to the meaning in a digital argument.

> We also want to reiterate Troy's main argument in *Crafting Digital Writing*:
> *It is one thing to fire off a status update, upload a quick snapshot, or post a*
> *hastily recorded video. It is quite another to craft a blog post linked from your*
> *update, compose a thoughtful photograph using the rule of thirds, or combine*
> *and edit multiple video clips to achieve a certain effect in a very brief film. It's*
> *all about intention and helping students identify, explore, and employ author's*
> *craft. (p. 19)*

In short, crafting digital arguments requires that writers understand and are able to use various forms of media to create arguments in a range of subgenres, or modes, of the argumentative form. In his previous books, Troy has used the MAPS framework to describe five components of a writing task. As with declarative and procedural knowledge, there is often a great deal of overlap when considering how these components interact. However, the MAPS heuristic provides a good starting point for conversations about specific writing tasks. In short, MAPS includes:

• Mode: the genre of a text. For our purposes, we are trying to distinguish between various subgenres of argument writing, such as op-ed columns, PSAs, and proposals.

- Media: the elements of form used to create a text, including alphabetic text, images, sounds, links, and videos.

- Audience: the reader, listener, or viewer of the text, both intended and incidental.

- Purpose: the goals of the writer in terms of substance, audience response, and writer's voice.

- Situation: the context for the writer, as well as the demands or constraints of the writing task.

At risk of overstating the point, the differentiation between mode and media is particularly important. We reiterate this idea because the many modes, or genres, of argument writing can be produced using various media. Therefore, we need to be quite explicit when teaching these ideas to our digital writers.

Why Teach Digital Arguments?

A distinct focus on teaching students how to craft digital arguments is useful for a variety of reasons.

First, we may be a bit idealistic, but we want students to be productive citizens and to use the opportunities available with digital writing for the greater good. Posting a selfie or retweeting someone else's post is one thing. Creating one's own valuable piece of writing that offers an argument of substance is quite another. We want students to create content, not just redistribute it. Or, to put it in terms used by digital literacy expert Doug Belshaw (2012), we want to move beyond "elegant consumption."

Second, practicing the *moves* of argument—with both print and digital writing—will help students become more proficient as critical thinkers. In recent years, scholars like Graff and Birkenstein (2009) and Joseph Harris (2006) have started describing these moves—or particular actions one can make in writing such as comparing, contrasting, extending, or rebutting—as ways that writers propel an argument forward. It is not enough, they suggest, to simply give writers strategies. Instead, as Harris notes, we as teachers must provide them with "a more dynamic vocabulary or action, gesture, and response" (p. 4). Using the language of the CCSS as a way to leverage conversations about good argument writing (claim, evidence, reason, counterclaim), we can help our students—and our colleagues—think critically, creatively, and carefully about when, how, and why to introduce the moves of digital argument in their curriculum. These digital moves, then, rely on both the language we introduce to our writers as well as the technical skills required to make certain actions occur in the context of digital writing (links to other websites, for instance).

While there are many critiques of the Common Core (and we have some of our own), we agree with Smith, Appleman, and Wilhelm (2014, p. 15): "Yes, there is much that is missing and potentially counterproductive about the CCSS . . . [but] it is up to us to fill the gaps—and we can fill the gaps." The CCSS do, in fact, demand that students "produce and publish" writing, "link to and cite sources," and "interact and collaborate" with others (National Governors Association 2010). It is our job to teach students how to accomplish these digital writing goals.

Third, we want students to be better writers in every part of their lives. We do so not just because the standards say so or because blue-ribbon reports urge us to create college- and career-ready writers. It may seem like a simple, perhaps naive goal, but we want for all children what we want for our own: successful and enjoyable literate lives. Students like Natalie—sometimes distracted by technology, sometimes in control of it—fill our classrooms, and we need to engage them in critical and creative opportunities for composing digital writing.

Finally, we agree with George Hillocks Jr.'s (1995) comment, "Argument is a basic structure of discourse that filters through everything we speak or write" (p. 129). Argument writing is not just one small portion of a yearly curriculum plan; it can—and should—be embedded throughout the entire year using different media. Nor is argument writing limited to ELA; it is a critical thinking skill that makes a difference across the curriculum and across the span of our students' lives.

More than ever before, students need intelligent, compassionate conversational partners, because conversations—some of which are truly interactive and dialogic, and others that are didactic and one-sided—are happening all around them, all the time. Teaching our students to craft digital arguments is, again, more than a skill for college or career. It is a skill for life. Building off the synergies of Kristen's work with argument (Turner 2005) and Troy's work with digital writing, we will deconstruct both professional and student arguments to delve into exactly how digital writing is different from print writing. Moreover, we will argue that teaching the mode of argument in both print and digital media is not an either/or choice. Instead, this is what many would call a "both/and," mainly because we know that crafting an argument through words is a necessary and complementary thinking process as students learn how to do the same in digital form.

As we move through the book, we will highlight how to teach these skills of digital argument so that students like Natalie can more adeptly consume the arguments they encounter and effectively produce their own arguments in the conversation that the Internet invites. Chapters 3 through 6 begin deconstructing the elements of argument in a variety of media, including blogs (Chapter 3), infographics (Chapter 4), videos (Chapter 5), and social media (Chapter 6). Each chapter will use the framework of declarative and procedural knowledge to break down the moves that digital writers make across these various forms of media. Chapter 7 will dig into assessment. Before we get to these ideas, though, Chapter 2 provides more background on the components of argument based in text, and how to connect those components to their digital equivalents.

A Brief Rationale for Teaching Digital Argument

1. To create productive citizens
2. To practice the moves of argument and develop critical thinking
3. To develop real-world literacy
4. To embed argument throughout the curriculum

ANALYZING ARGUMENTS THAT ARE BORN DIGITAL

Argument can take many forms. Literary analyses, position papers, and mathematical proofs represent traditional academic arguments. As Lunsford, Ruszkiewicz, and Walters (2013) remind us, arguments also surround us every day. Billboards, flyers, and book jackets can all be forms of argument. More and more often, our daily lives exist within digital spaces—and digital arguments abound.

In thinking about more traditional forms of argument, Hillocks (1995, 2011) suggested that we, as teachers, need to define the strategies that enable writers to produce arguments. As we analyze digital arguments in this light, we recognize that some of these strategies mirror exactly what Hillocks identified—namely, the need to understand how claims, evidence, and warrants work together to make an argument. However, digital texts require additional strategies. If we want students to be able to read and write digital arguments, we need to develop their procedural knowledge as it relates, specifically, to the moves of digital argument across various modes and media. Our work is not about having students merely "create a blog," "produce a podcast," or "develop a video." Rather, it is about exploring the technological opportunities that allow writers to craft digital arguments—and how the technology allows readers to engage with these texts so that students can read and write these texts in real time in their real lives, as compared to the inauthentic tasks they are often assigned in school.

In this chapter, we'll consider how to teach students to read and write arguments that are *born digital*, building on what Hillocks articulated by considering the features of these kinds of texts and by expanding students' procedural knowledge of form and substance.

"Born Digital" Arguments

The term *born digital* was popularized in 2008 with Palfrey and Gasser's book *Born Digital: Understanding the First Generation of Digital Natives*. It referred specifically to the generation of children born after 1980 who were brought up with ubiquitous screens and the emergence of the Internet. In this chapter, however, we are referring to "born digital" *items,* not people. Ricky Erway (2010) of the Online Computer Library Center defines "born digital" items as those "created and managed in digital form." Included in this broad description are digital photographs, manuscripts, harvested web pages, data sets, electronic records, art, games, and other items that have been created in a digital format and designed for consumption on a digital device.

To help put into perspective the difference between traditional print text (which may be translated to screen through a PDF), and born digital text, consider one of the most traditional print forms of argument, a letter to a newspaper editor, alongside today's digital arguments. In the late 1990s, Kristen used letters to the editor from the local paper to introduce her students to the idea of analyzing arguments. The letters were short, sometimes only a sentence or two, and did not allow for immediate response from readers. Though the teens found great satisfaction in dissecting poorly written claims that were usually not supported by evidence, their critiques did not—and in fact, could not—reach the authors.

Today, however, students can critique the equivalent of a letter to the editor on nearly any personal blog, in the comments on news articles, and in "opinion" sections on news websites. Without space constraints, these arguments tend to be longer than those published in the local paper. In addition, they can use hyperlinks, videos, and images to support the opinions. Even more interesting, however, is the fact that anyone—including students—can instantly respond to the author of the piece.

Letters to the editor in the newspaper are very different from the hyperlinked arguments that today's adolescents encounter on a daily basis in a digital world. With the ability for anyone to publish comes a responsibility for readers to think

critically about what they are reading, and students today must consider how writers use media to assert their arguments. A savvy reader needs to learn how to deconstruct these born digital arguments.

Considering Hyperlinks

Texts that include hyperlinks are born digital since they must be read on a screen to get the full effect of the author's work: the arguments that are embedded in a text depend, in large part, on the links. To illustrate just how much hyperlinks matter, in Figure 2.1 we offer three versions of hyperlinks for the same sentence

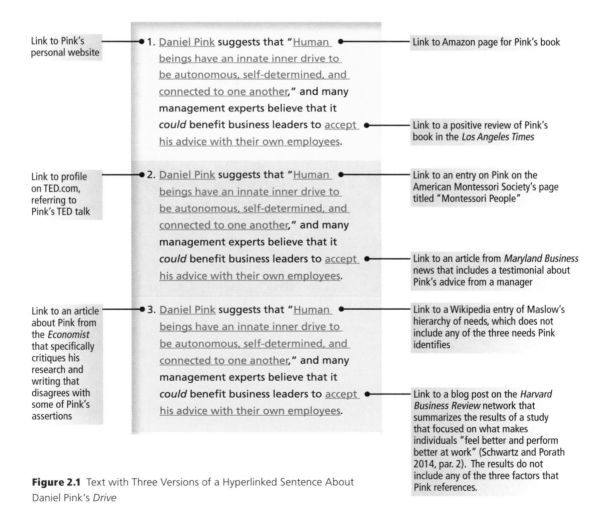

Figure 2.1 Text with Three Versions of a Hyperlinked Sentence About Daniel Pink's *Drive*

about Daniel Pink and an argument he makes in his 2011 book, *Drive: The Surprising Truth About What Motivates Us*. (If you are reading the print version of this book, you can rely on the descriptions on this page, or you might pause now to go to our companion wiki to try this reading experience for yourself. If you're reading an ebook that has an Internet connection, click on the links to follow them. The website will contain updated links. Those referenced in this book were active as of July 2016.)

As you explore the three versions of the sentence, consider the following:

- Where does each of the links lead?

- How do you think the writer chose those links?

- Considering the rhetorical situation, *why* do you think the writer chose the links? Notice that the writer italicized the word "could" in each statement. What goal is he/she trying to accomplish by using the links, and how does it relate to the word "could" being italicized?

- For you, as a reader, are the links effective? Do they work well with the claim being made? Why or why not?

An analysis of these paragraphs will reveal that the arguments made in each of the three versions are distinctly different, giving a different shade of nuance to the italicized word "could," but you'll learn this only by following the hyperlinks. In this sense, the links themselves serve as both evidence and warrant, without much in the way of an elaborate explanation.

In the first version, the links we have found through a basic web search serve as evidence that Daniel Pink is an expert, thus helping to create an implied warrant: "If an expert suggests it, we should take the advice." The use of italics on the word "could," in this case, makes us think of potential, of possibility, and the links back up this argument.

In the second version, we have expanded our web search, going deeper to uncover new evidence to support our argument, and in the process, we have complicated the argument being made. Though we rely on Pink's quotation in our stated text, the rhetorical move we make with the hyperlink provides a questioning reader with additional evidence to support the claim. In moving beyond the top three links on a Google search, we have found other kinds of evidence, which we incorporated

Classroom Example: What's Up with School Lunch?

While we find the Daniel Pink example useful in certain contexts (e.g., workshops with teachers, AP sociology or psychology classes), we recognize that it is not engaging to most students. However, this type of analysis can be done with students using texts and topics relevant to them. For instance, in Lauren King's New York City classroom (@MsKingNYC), her tenth graders were often vocal about their school lunches, and she used the three sentences in Figure 2.2 in an activity designed to get them to think carefully about hyperlinks. Based on an activity that Troy designed for professional development work with teachers, each of the three paragraphs contains the same text, but with different links.

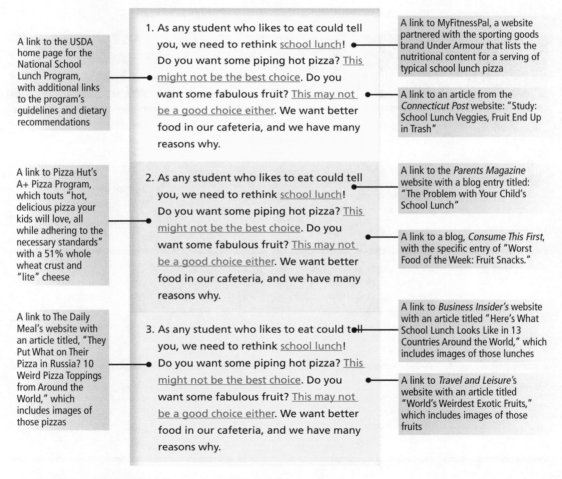

Figure 2.2 Student Text with Three Versions of Hyperlinks

Instructions for Students

Read the examples. The sentences in each numbered paragraph are the same, but they have different hyperlinks. Go through each version one at a time and analyze the sites being used.

As you analyze each hyperlink jot down why it works, or why it doesn't. Explain your reasoning.

Lauren shared a document in Google Classroom so that each student could complete a chart analyzing the links. In Table 2.1, we represent some of the students' ideas through a composite of paraphrased responses. We will refer to this student as Tomas.

Table 2.1 Tomas' Responses to the School Lunch Hyperlinks

Hyperlink:	"school lunch"	"This might not be the best choice"	"This may not be a good choice either"
Version 1	Well it explains how school lunch works in the education system. We are supplied with a "nutritionally balanced meal," according to the NSLP. Not the best link	Shows the nutritional value of a slice of school pizza. Not the best choice of food because provides very little health value. Decent link	According to a Harvard study, 40% of fruits in school lunch are thrown out. Better than the first two hyperlinks. Decent link
Version 2	School lunch is not as healthy as it is claims to be. High-fat, high-sodium and low-fiber meal. Decent link	Link contradicts statement of pizza not being a good idea by linking to a Pizza Hut page . . . Bad link	Bad link. Links to an article on fruit SNACKS instead of actual fresh fruits.
Version 3	Link doesn't work because it's comparing school lunches from other countries to ours.	Link not worthy. Links to an article on Russia and what they use as topping for pizza.	BAD link. Links to a gallery of exotic fruits. Has absolutely nothing to do with school lunch.

Which sentence was the most convincing? Why?
- Version 2, school lunch hyperlink. Gives good reason as to why school lunch is not as healthy as it claims to be.

The day before this lesson, to get Tomas and his classmates thinking about their reading habits and how hyperlinks can lead them from one text to another, Lauren asked the students to play the hyperlink game Wikispeedia. The game requires players to attempt to move between two randomly generated topics on *Wikipedia* using only the hyperlinks within *Wikipedia*. For example, players must move from something like "football" to "mitosis" in as few clicks as possible. As described by West et al. (2009), the purpose of the activity is to demonstrate that

> the raw hyperlink structure of Wikipedia leads to several problems. First, while many hyperlinks correspond to semantic links, many others do not. Links are often added based on the inclination of the author, rather than because the concepts are related. Also, if one looks only at the presence or absence of links, no distinction can be made between closely and loosely related concepts. This leads to a combinatorial explosion, such that every page is connected to every other page by 4.6 links on average. (p. 1598)

Thus, links alone are not always the best way to determine useful connections between ideas, and the game is meant to illustrate that point.

As they worked, students cheered when they were successful and groaned when they failed. During their debrief of this lesson, Tomas commented: "Some of the things I read made me curious to read more." But if a link brought him to a random site, he responded, "I totally don't care anymore." This personal reflection on his reading habits, sparked by the Wikispeedia game, helped him to consider the links in the school lunch task. Of the three arguments presented, his assessment was that the second version of the school lunch sentence was the best.

Interestingly enough, the conversation about the link to Pizza Hut sparked even more discussion among students in the class. Was this writer trying to demonstrate that he was against having Pizza Hut pizza served in schools, even though the company website claimed that it was "healthy"? Or was the writer attempting to be sarcastic, demonstrating that he really liked Pizza Hut and would want to eat that instead of typical school pizza? The connotation of the words in the hyperlinked sentence—"Do you want some piping hot pizza? This might not be the best choice"—was not clear, and the link, in turn, didn't make the writer's intended meaning any clearer. ■

into our argument without changing the language of the sentence (or paragraph). Here, use of the word "could" seems to imply that the writer herself is still questioning whether Pink's advice would work, yet the links suggest that it will.

Finally, in the third example of the sentence, the links reveal a different set of assumptions about who Daniel Pink is and the credibility that he brings to this conversation.

So what are we saying with this final example? Perhaps we are writing sarcastically. Or perhaps we are introducing a counterargument to a different claim. The use of "could" in italics here suggests a different shade of meaning; it is not about potential or inquiry and is, instead, about doubt. No matter the author intent, her argument here is much different from the first two—all because of the rhetorical use of hyperlinked content.

Digital texts that include hyperlinks pose unique challenges to readers and writers as they consider the roles of claim, evidence, and warrant in their arguments. In the example (p.21), we can see how a student could employ links to make three very different kinds of arguments and, consequently, it raises questions about the teaching needed to help students introduce, insert, and interpret various links (just like quotes from other sources).

Considering Images

Similarly, digital arguments that use images, like the one in Figure 2.3, allow writers to use various media to marshal evidence, underscore claims, provide warrants, and acknowledge rebuttals. In this post, we can identify a clear claim: "[It is a] great night for the firemen's carnival." This claim is supported by the image of Kristen's children, smiling in front of a carnival ride. With the sun shining in the background, clear sky above and lush green grass below, the image itself argues that the weather is perfect and the children are happy, and the post, without specifically stating it, invites others in the community to join the event.

This simple argument resembles many posts made on social media, and though it is likely that readers and

Great night for the firemen's carnival

Figure 2.3 A Post from Kristen's Facebook Page

writers in these spaces do not often think about them as arguments, image and video play key roles in making and supporting claims.

Other digital arguments are more complex. For example, in the blog post cited in Chapter 1, "Dear parents, you are being lied to," Kristen was drawn to the title *and* the image of the post (p. 2), which she encountered on her friend's social media stream. The image of the smiling mom, who holds her sleeve so that her child can "play doctor" and pretend to administer a needle in her upper arm, supports the overall claim made by the author: "You don't need to be afraid of vaccines."

Gateway Activities for Digital Arguments

Sitting among the professional texts on Kristen's bookshelf, three books—*You're The Detective* (Treat 1983), *Crime and Puzzlement* (Treat 1981), and *Two-Minute Mysteries* (Sobol 1967)—seem out of place. Why would books of mini-mysteries be among her teaching resources?

The answer comes from the work of George Hillocks Jr., who inspired Kristen to rethink her teaching of both reading and writing in order to focus on helping students develop skills of argumentation. His book *Teaching Argument Writing, Grades 6–12* describes activities that use mini-mysteries to help "students learn the strategies for making arguments" (2011, p. 16). He lists these four strategies:

- analyzing evidence in light of existing knowledge

- interpreting the evidence to explain what it shows

- developing warrants [or statements of connection] that show why the evidence is relevant [to the claim]

- using the evidence and the explanations to solve the problem [that is presented] (p. 16)

For Hillocks, articulating the strategies of writing argument is the key to understanding the instruction that we, as teachers, need to provide. Hillocks believed that the activities we choose "have to involve students in appropriate strategies of inquiry and ways of generating discourse features" such as those just listed (1995, p. 149). He suggested the invention of "gateway activities" to "engage students in using difficult production strategies with varying levels of support" (p. 149), eventually leading them to independent writing of arguments.

Gateway activities must pose a problem that captures students' attention, as well as allow students to grapple with the problem and to collect (or uncover) data that helps them to do so; ultimately, they are able to develop arguable positions. Kristen's mentor, Michael Smith, would add that they should be designed as arguments "in miniature." In other words, gateway activities are highly engaging tasks that prepare students to create longer, extended arguments by helping them develop discrete strategies that make up the discourse of argument. They are not, however, the "steps" of writing an argumentative essay (e.g., brainstorming, outlining). In this sense, they are generative, not prescriptive.

Hillocks (2011) details several gateway activities for helping students develop strategies that they will need to produce arguments. Kristen has used nearly all of them with middle and high school students over the last two decades. In this chapter, we provide a range of gateway activities for digital arguments that, like those Hillocks originally devised, help students to work on skills in miniature. These activities help students to explore some of the features and strategies unique to digital arguments:

- using images to make a claim

- using images as evidence

- evaluating evidence

- refining criteria for evaluation

- responding to counterclaims

- attending to fonts, layouts, and other design elements

Each of these strategies is essential to reading and writing digital arguments, and we, like Hillocks, recommend that teachers provide students with a number of engaging, inquiry-based activities that focus on the skills in isolation, rather than creating long, drawn-out projects that require mastery of the skills in steps. In this way, teachers can build upon the skills students will need in a variety of contexts, rather than focusing on one final product. In the following sections we describe one example activity for each skill, with hopes that it will inspire you to create additional ones of your own (and share them on our wiki).

Using Images to Make a Claim

Though *Wikipedia* defines *meme* as "an image, behavior, or style that spreads from person to person," the term *meme* has been used colloquially to refer to images that are overlaid with text and shared on the Internet.

Because of the current popularity of memes, Kristen chose to use them as the subject of her lesson with a third-grade class. After asking the children to brainstorm about "what writing is" and sharing with them responses to this same prompt that their parents, grandparents, and older siblings had written on a Google doc, she showed them memes that had been created using quotations from famous authors. For about ten minutes, the class perused "data" that would help them to formulate opinions about "what writing is."

One of the memes Kristen selected used a quote from Henry Miller—"Writing, like life itself, is a voyage of discovery"—paired with an aerial image of a mountain range bordered by two valleys.

> "Why do you think the creator used this particular image?" Kristen asked the class.
> "Because it's like you're in an airplane," one boy responded.
> "Yeah, and you can see different things, like discover them," his classmate added.
> "What about this word *voyage*?" Kristen prompted. "Does anyone know what *voyage* means?"
> "Like a trip on a ship," came a voice from the back of the room.
> "That's great!" Kristen replied. "Can we connect *voyage* to *airplane*?"

Through the conversation, Kristen led the children to understand that the creator of the meme selected the image to complement the quotation—to underscore the claim that writing is a voyage of discovery. To have kids practice the strategy of pairing images with words to make a clear claim, she then asked pairs to make their own claims about writing, using images and words and the iPad app Mematic.

The children first completed one of the following sentences: "Writing is _____" or "Writing helps me _____." Then in pairs they negotiated the claim they wanted to make and spent several minutes searching, filtering, and discarding before selecting the perfect image to support their assertion. Kristen monitored the discussions and prompted students to consider how the images supported their claims, asking questions like, "Why do you think that image is the best choice?"

Ryan and Cole, the creators of the meme shown in Figure 2.4, struggled at first to find an appropriate image that represented the word *everything*. Kristen passed by their table and noticed their struggle.

Kristen: How's it going?

Ryan: We can't decide on a picture.

Kristen: Well, what is your claim about writing?

Cole: Writing is everything.

Kristen: What kind of picture would be "everything"?

Ella (a student at their table)**:** We've been trying to help them figure that out.

Ryan: Yeah, we've been thinking about searching the earth.

Cole: But we have this picture of space.

Kristen: Well, which do you think best shows "everything"?

Ella and Olivia (simultaneously)**:** Space.

Ryan: Yeah, space.

Kristen: Why do you think that? Why don't you and Cole talk about that, and I'll be back to see what you decided.

Figure 2.4 "Writing Is Everything" Meme

When Kristen returned to the pair, they eagerly showed her their final product, with Cole exclaiming, "Space is everything. Not the earth!!" Their decision to use a picture of space came after discussion with each other, their peers, and the teacher. Their selection of the image was intentional and clearly articulated their claim.

Using Images as Evidence

To introduce the idea that images can serve as evidence, Sheila Cooperman (@Sheila Cooperman), a middle school teacher in Connecticut, brings in print magazines for her sixth-grade students and asks them to find an advertisement that they find interesting. The children work in pairs to analyze the ad by answering the following questions:

• What is this advertisement saying?

• How do you know?

As the students share their selected ads, Sheila pushes their thinking about the evidence they are citing to support what the advertisement says. She keeps track on the board when a group points to words in the ad and when they point to images. After everyone has shared, she notes that the advertisements used both words and images as evidence to support the claim. Then she challenges students to find two more ads that use images as evidence.

Sheila's activity introduces students to the idea of image as evidence, a concept she expects them to use when they write digital arguments later in the year. One of her students produced the argument shown in Figure 2.5 as part of that later project. This student made the implied claim that readers of the image should not do drugs. His evidence, given in the form of an image, includes physi-

Figure 2.5 "Don't Let This Be You" Meme

cal effects, and it links to the claim through an implied warrant: negative changes in body image are not worth it.

By using the two key questions above repeatedly in her discussion with students, Sheila is able to reinforce that evidence answers the question, "How do you know?" and is distinct from the use of images to make a claim, described in the preceding section.

Evaluating Evidence

Toulmin, Rieke, and Janik (1979) suggested that disciplines value different kinds of evidence. For example, they suggested that hard sciences lean toward statistical data, whereas courts of law often prioritize first-person, anecdotal evidence. Effective arguments make use of the evidence that their audiences value. In digital arguments, writers need to choose not only the type of evidence appropriate for their audience, but also the best medium to present that evidence. There's no shortage of options: an expert's opinion, for instance, could come in the form of a video interview with the person, a podcast produced by the expert, an infographic that summarizes the individual's research, a hyperlink to a blog written by the expert, or even alphabetic text that quotes another source. So how do authors choose both their evidence and the medium to present it? And how do readers recognize the role this medium plays in shaping (and sharing) the argument?

To engage students in thinking about these questions, we suggest introducing them briefly to some of the types of evidence typically associated with debate: scientific law, statistical data, expert opinion, opinion of noted individuals, and anecdotal evidence. Kristen was introduced to these categories many years ago by her department supervisor in a faculty meeting that focused on debate in the classroom, and has successfully used the following descriptions to help students think carefully about what counts as evidence in various contexts. After sharing these categories, explain to students that they will be looking for a variety of evidence as they conduct their own inquiries and evaluating its importance to their opinions about their topics.

Common Types of Evidence

Scientific law—proven facts that are considered basically indisputable. For example, one cannot really argue that men and women have different physical attributes. Additionally, one cannot argue that the laws of gravity don't apply to all objects within the earth's atmosphere. This kind of evidence sometimes provides the fundamental basis for an argument and serves as its own warrant.

Statistical data—the results of controlled studies. Figures can be manipulated to support different conclusions, but the data itself is objective.

Expert opinion—the opinion of an individual or group that has studied data, law, or a specific discipline where expertise is recognized. This evidence is open to dispute because experts differ in their conclusions and some people are considered more expert than others.

Opinion of a noted individual—the opinion of a person whose character and opinions have grown to be trusted. This opinion carries weight because of the "celebrity" status. For example, a respected news reporter may not be an expert on the issues on which he or she reports, but people's trust in the reporter makes his or her opinions powerful.

Anecdotal evidence—a single example that is used to prove a point. For example, one might say, "I know that cigarette smoking causes cancer because my aunt got cancer from smoking." This kind of evidence often has an emotional appeal.

Then, further to define the inquiries, we recommend borrowing an activity from Daniels and Ahmed (2014) that will tap into students' curiosities. Begin with a three-minute brainstorm where students list topics that they are curious about. Their questions can be personal, such as, "Why are my eyes blue?" or more global, like, "Will humans ever live on another planet?"

After three minutes, students pair up and share their lists, looking for overlapping curiosities. Together they craft one question for the day's inquiry and prepare to find a source that helps to answer the question. As you model the process for them, share your own inquiry question and Internet search. Conduct a think-aloud as you focus on the type of source you have found (e.g., article, video, infographic) and the kinds of evidence presented in each source, using the graphic organizer in Figure 2.6 to document your thinking.

Students should try to find evidence that represents at least two different forms of media and at least two different types of evidence. You might make a game of the task by challenging students to check off each type of evidence and each form of media in Figure 2.7.

As a culmination, ask pairs to share the piece of evidence they found most compelling to their question and to comment on the type of evidence and the medium and how those aspects played into their comments. How did *this* evidence and *this* medium reach *this* audience well?

Evidence Note-Taking Sheet for Curiosity Inquiries

Name: _____ Class: _____ Date: _____

Considering Sources

Inquiry Question: _____

Source Title, Author, Web Address	Evidence What fact or quotation did you find?	Type of Evidence Scientific law, statistics, expert opinion, noted individual, anecdotal	Media Video, audio, infographic, hyperlink to another site, text only	Your Comment What is the value of this evidence *and* this media to your inquiry question?

Figure 2.6 Evidence Note-Taking Sheet for Curiosity Inquiries

© 2017 by Kristen Hawley Turner and Troy Hicks from *Argument in the Real World*. Portsmouth, NH: Heinemann.

Name: _____   Class: _____   Date: _____

Evidence Checklist

Type of Evidence		Form of Media	
☐	Scientific Law	☐	Video
☐	Statistics	☐	Audio
☐	Expert Opinion	☐	Infographic
☐	Opinion of Noted Individual	☐	Hyperlink to Another Site
☐	Anecdotal Evidence	☐	Text Only

Figure 2.7 Evidence Checklist

© 2017 by Kristen Hawley Turner and Troy Hicks from *Argument in the Real World*. Portsmouth, NH: Heinemann.

Using Criteria for Evaluation

Anyone with a social media feed reads examples of weak arguments as their friends and followers share emotional opinions without support for their claims. As Hillocks claimed, "[S]tudents . . . may think rightly that a policy is unfair, but most students do not articulate the *reasons* that it is unfair; when they do, they use simplistic criteria" (2006, p. 41). In fact, the Internet is full of arguments of judgment and policy where the authors have not articulated reasons or used relatively simple criteria for them. Teaching students to define (and identify) the criteria to evaluate a digital argument may help temper a mass spewing of unsubstantiated judgments that can be destructive to society.

Alex Corbitt (@Alex_Corbitt), a middle school teacher in New York City, has extended Hillocks' work by helping students define and evaluate criteria in the digital realm. Inspired by Kelly Gallagher's *Write Like This* (2011), Alex challenges his students to write Amazon.com reviews and publish them on the website. First, students choose a personal item, one that they value and can easily evaluate. Next, they establish criteria for their evaluation. If, for example, they're considering beanbag chairs, the criteria might include how comfortable the chair is, the durability of the cover, and the overall appearance. Like Gallagher, Alex uses exemplar Amazon.com reviews as mentor texts to help his students see that explicitly stating criteria allows writers to compare products against similar items on the market. These are the steps the students followed:

Steps for Writing an Amazon.com Review

1. Choose a personal item that you value.

2. Establish criteria for evaluation.

3. Rate the item on a 1 to 5 scale in each of the categories.

4. Qualify the ratings (i.e., why did it receive 4 out of 5 rather than 5 out of 5?).

5. Provide a "bottom line" judgment about the product that takes into account all of the criteria.

6. Publish the review on Amazon.com.

Like her classmates, Elizabeth engaged quickly in the assignment. She selected an iPad Air as her personal item of value and identified the following criteria for evaluation: design, apps, camera, and colors. Then she followed Alex's instructions to rate the device in each of these categories on a scale of 1 to 5. This process requires nuanced thinking that moves away from either/or mentalities of "good" and "bad." Elizabeth's final review (see Figure 2.8) included the pros and cons in each category before giving her overall judgment: "Even though there might be some problems with this tablet (such as the apps lagging/glitching), it's still a good product." Her qualified ratings of the device in each category supported this conclusion.

Alex posted the review on Elizabeth's behalf because she did not have an active Amazon account, and almost immediately it received feedback from the community. Elizabeth was excited to see other Amazon.com users rate her review as "helpful." The assignment gave her and her classmates the opportunity to receive meaningful, honest, real-world feedback on their writing. Alex encourages them to respond to questions and pointed counterclaims. The students take pride in belonging to a digital community, and the activity engages them as they learn how to define and articulate criteria for their judgments.

Anticipating and Responding to Counterclaims

When Kristen taught high school, she was frustrated by her students' academic writing skills. Each year their research papers presented arguments that were entirely one-sided. Rarely did a student rebut a counterclaim—or even acknowledge that another position might exist. When she made debate a regular part of her classroom, however, her students' writing changed. As they became more comfortable countering each other in face-to-face conversations, they began to incorporate counterclaims into their writing. Debate helped them to develop procedural knowledge of rebuttal.

Debate is still a strong tool in teaching argument writing. However, in a world of social media, we have a range of new tools at our disposal. Careful reading of arguments in social media shows that the ability to respond to counterclaims with decorum

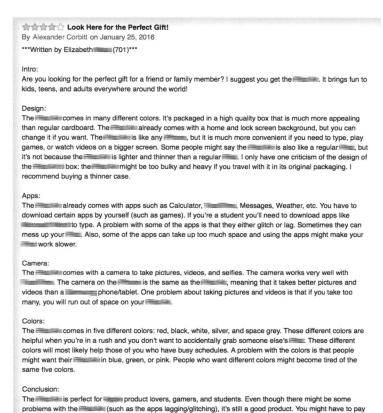

Figure 2.8 "Look Here for the Perfect Gift!" Review

sets apart thoughtful, mindful individuals from a mass of knee-jerk reactors. If you have read YouTube or Amazon reviews, you may find yourself trusting authors who counter alternative views carefully. For instance, last summer when Kristen's husband was searching for a vacation rental, he scoured properties on VRBO (Vacation Rental by Owner). Though he was interested in what the renters had to say about the homes, he paid close attention to how owners responded to renters' claims. In one case, he discarded a home with close to five-star reviews simply because the owner reacted emotionally, rather than logically, to a negative comment about the property.

To highlight the power of social media to provide a real audience and to help his students learn to anticipate and respond to counterclaims, Alex (the middle school teacher in the previous section) uses Yelp.com in the classroom. First he has students read Yelp reviews and investigate the author's reliability. They ask questions like these:

- Who is this person?
- What information can I find on their Yelp profile?
- What other reviews has this person written?
- Are they inconsistent in their judgments?
- Do they seem to be biased?

In addition to the reliability of the writer, the students also consider how anecdotal and photographic evidence contribute to the quality of a review. Once they have considered reviews posted by others, Alex has his students review local shops and restaurants around the school community, considering the counterclaims that might be made. For example, Jamie, a seventh grader, reviewed a local sportswear and shoe store, Jimmy Jazz (see Figure 2.9).

In her review, she provided evidence to support several claims; but perhaps even more important, she addressed a potential counterpoint. In her first full paragraph, she stated, "Some of their shoes come in a limited variety of sizes," before going on to assert that the selection is so extensive that "you will definitely find a style you love!" Like Kristen's students, who envisioned responses to their arguments in a debate, Jamie was able to consider alternative views and incor-

Figure 2.9 Jamie Working on Her Yelp Review (Photo by Alex)

porate them into her writing (see Figure 2.10).

Because Yelp small business owners tend to be more socially engaged than the large companies featured on Amazon, Alex's students often receive quick responses to their posted reviews. If their claims and evidence are challenged, students can investigate the reliability of the author and, if appropriate, formulate rebuttals to defend their positions.

By engaging in this authentic space, students can create change in their communities, and they can develop skills of rebuttal that extend beyond the classroom walls and their academic writing.

Jimmy Jazz
218 E 161st Street
Bronx, NY 10451

★★★★★ 2/8/2016

🔔 First to Review

Written By Jamie ▓▓▓(702)

Are you looking for new shoes and sportswear? Well, Jimmy Jazz is the place to go! They have great products for spectacular prices!

Jimmy Jazz's shoes are amazing. They are comfortable, fashionable, and colorful (excellent for kids). Some of their shoes come in a limited variety of sizes. Don't worry, though, they have such a huge shoe selection. You will definitely find a style that you love. The biggest problem is that there are so many great pairs of shoes to choose from!

Jimmy Jazz's clothes are amazing because they are stylish and affordable. The clothes are made of quality materials and are durable in any weather condition. Jimmy Jazz always sells their clothes at lower prices than their competitors. If you are ever trying to find clothes for you or a loved one, Jimmy Jazz is definitely the place to go.

The employees at Jimmy Jazz are very kind and enthusiastic. They greet you when you enter the store and give you a heartwarming smile. When you ask for help they happily assist you. The employees are patient no matter what, even if you spend a long time looking around the store. I have always felt very comfortable around the staff no matter what.

If I didn't have Jimmy Jazz, then I wouldn't be able to find the apparel I need! Jimmy Jazz should be in more cities across the country. More people should be able to experience Jimmy Jazz and their professional employees!

Figure 2.10 Jamie's Yelp Review

Arguing with Graphic Design: Fonts, Layouts, and Color

The meme that Ryan and Cole created to state their claim that "writing is everything" borrowed an image that had been crafted purposefully. The image they remixed was the photo of the earth, with the moon in the upper corner, and the word *everything* in the middle. In creating this image, the authors attended to the "rule of thirds," highlighting the word *everything*, perhaps as a claim that the earth is not the center of the universe. Additionally, the Star Wars font serves as a cultural touchstone that invokes the idea that there are galaxies "far, far away," further supporting the claim. These choices, we think, were not accidental. The composition of the image makes an argument.

As third graders, Ryan and Cole likely did not think about these aspects of their own argument, but novice readers and writers must learn how fonts, layouts, and color help to craft a digital argument.

Betsy Reid (@readBReid), a twelfth-grade English teacher in Richmond, Virginia, has done this work with her high school students using logos. She begins with a discussion of the school logo, shown in Figure 2.11, and provides the following prompt: "At some point, the leaders of this school sat down together with a job to do: they needed to come up with a logo to reflect what this school is all about. Think about all of the design elements of this logo. What do you think each of these elements is saying about this school?"

Figure 2.11
Betsy's School Logo

During the discussion, her students articulated that the three crosses at the top of the logo represent the Father, Son, and Holy Spirit and therefore assert the Episcopalian background of the school. The use of the lower half of a cross serves two purposes: to bolster the upper three crosses, giving them a prominent position, and to reflect the edge of the markings of a sports field, which is also one of the cornerstones of the school. Additionally, students noticed the subtle color differences with the blue outline and green fill, the school colors. Finally, they commented on the shape of the logo. For them, the shield shape (as opposed to a circle or square) represented power, defense against aggression, and tradition.

Figure 2.12
Twitter Logo

After introducing her students to the idea that visual elements make arguments, Betsy engaged them with analysis of high-interest logos: Twitter (shown in Figure 2.12), Amazon, and Snapchat. She asked the students to consider how the companies designed an image to make "an argument to the world in one symbol."

Betsy then passed out a recognizable logo to each small group in her classroom and asked them to discuss the company, its mission, and its background. To help students analyze the logo, she prompted them to consider the following questions:

- How does the color contribute to the message?

- What shape is used and why?

- If applicable, how is text displayed (consider font and placement) and what effect does it have?

- What elements of the overall layout contribute to the argument being made?

The small group that focused on the Twitter logo noted that the bird looks like he is in motion, just like a Twitter feed, and that the beak is open, perhaps singing to the world, just as the purpose of Twitter is to share a person's voice. They also discussed the angle of the bird's beak: the upward trajectory indicates a positive force. The students felt that Twitter itself was a positive flow of information, especially for inspiring social change, and that the company would not want to create a logo that would reflect the negative aspects of Twitter. Finally, they noted that the color blue, first associated with Facebook, has become a representative color of social media.

As students uncovered possible claims being made in these logos, they began to see how font, color, and layout contribute as evidence and warrants for these claims, and they became invested in deeper analysis.

Betsy then turned their attention to political logos. With the 2016 presidential primary race under way, she used an article from the *Washington Post*, "Which 2016 Presidential Candidate Has the Worst Logo?" (Strals and Willen 2015), as the basis for her lesson. She began not by distributing the article but by handing out printed images of the candidates' logos discussed in the article. She asked students to predict the candidates' platforms based on the images, fonts, color, and layouts of their logos. She noticed that many groups pulled out devices to investigate campaign websites, and as they shared their graphics and predictions with the class, they were able to link the visual aspects of the logo to ideas like "conservative," "liberal," "forward-thinking," and "representative of minority groups." Table 2.2 shows the analysis of the Trump and Clinton logos done by Betsy's students during this activity.

Table 2.2 Student Analysis of the Trump and Clinton Logos

Trump Logo 	Clinton Logo
• All about the name. • All caps = strong name recognition. • Strong font reflects his persona and the fact that the campaign is about HIM and by HIM (self-funded, no advisors). • Font resembles his own business brand, which most people recognize, and makes the claim that Trump is America. • Tagline—assumes America is not great. • Exclamation mark reflects enthusiasm and confidence, claiming it's his mission.	• Red, white, and blue colors highlight the arrow, which means it is important. • Arrow points forward to represent the idea of moving forward—compared to Obama's sun rise in the middle of the O, this visual suggests a shift from a new day to forward progress. • Arrow pointing right may indicate that she is not as far left as she is portrayed and that she can represent all people. • "Font" design is strong and bold, representing Clinton.

For homework, students read the *Washington Post* article and reflected on the following question: How does each image use color, fonts, and layout in a way that reveals the brand/beliefs of the candidate? This activity helped them to develop procedural knowledge of arguing through graphic design.

We can further help students to consider the uses and effects of graphic design by helping them to understand the *principles* of graphic design. There are countless resources about graphic design, a few of which we will introduce later in the book. For the moment, however, we mention the work of Robin Williams, a graphic designer whose *Non-designer's Design Book*, now in its fourth edition, offers a simple set of criteria on which to base effective designs: contrast, repetition, alignment, and proximity (frequently referred to by their acronym, CRAP).

She defines the four principles as follows (2014, p. 13):

- Contrast: "The idea behind contrast is to avoid elements on the page that are merely *similar*. If the elements (type, color, size, line thickness, shape, space, etc.) are not the *same*, then make them **very different**." (Emphasis in original)

- Repetition: "Repeat visual elements of the design throughout the piece . . . This develops the organization and strengthens the unity." She lists many examples, as she did for contrast, and also includes font and graphic concepts.

- Alignment: "Nothing should be placed on the page arbitrarily. Every element should have some visual connection with another element on the page." This can include alignment with hard and fast lines or shapes, or implied, invisible lines.

- Proximity: "Items related to each other should be grouped close together. When several items are in close proximity to each other, they become one visual unit rather than several separate units." Again, this can include any visual element.

In sum, Williams argues that designers use these principles in tandem to create the most effective visuals, and we see this work of viewing (like reading and listening) and visually representing (like writing and speaking) to be equally important as we teach students how to craft digital arguments. As students consider how designers use contrast, repetition, alignment, and proximity, they may be able to see the designer's point of view or purpose more clearly.

Looking Ahead

In this chapter, we have discussed how knowledge of argument—knowledge of claims, evidence, warrants, and rebuttals—is something all writers need. Argument is just as present in digital media as it is in traditional written prose. However, digital arguments also give writers options such as links, video, audio, and graphics, all of which can serve in their own right as elements of a given argument. The wider range of modes in digital writing adds yet another layer of craft to the writing process: the difference between an op-ed letter and a public service announcement, for instance. In other words, writing a blog post is a different task than composing a digital video or an infographic, and it behooves us to figure out what moves writers can make to craft arguments within (and across) each type of media.

The suggestions in this chapter will help you lay the groundwork for critically reading and writing digital arguments with your students by developing their procedural knowledge. In the next three chapters, we will examine arguments in web-based texts, infographics, and videos, focusing specifically on the strategies needed to compose and consume these texts. Then in Chapter 6, we will consider how social media can be seen as a space for reading and writing arguments. Finally, in Chapter 7 we will discuss issues of assessment.

CHAPTER 3

THE MOVES OF ARGUMENT IN WEB-BASED TEXT

A few years ago, Rebekah Shoaf (@rlshoaf), an instructional coach in New York City, asked her students to move their independent reading journals from print notebooks to web-based texts. Students maintained their responses to their reading on an individual page on the class wiki, where all the other students in the class could view it.

Alexandra's wiki page, shown in Figure 3.1, exemplifies what Rebekah describes as "publishing, not crafting" a digital text. At the time, Rebekah was most concerned about having her students share their reading in a convenient online space, and providing opportunities for them to comment on one another's responses to the books that they shared. Each entry in Alexandra's online reading journal appears in a different color, underneath the book jacket image of *The Perks of Being a Wallflower*, by Stephen Chbosky. Over the course of two weeks, Alexandra used her journal to explore the idea of being "feminine" as compared to being a "feminist." A few classmates commented on her entries, and she commented in return.

Reflecting on the assignment now, Rebekah acknowledges, "When I started that process, I wasn't worried about how they were crafting; I was just having them write digitally what they would have written in their journals." In this sense, they had moved their reading response from a notebook to the class website housed on

The Perks of Being a Wallflower &
The difference between being Feminine and being Feminist

11.01.12

In this post, I will try to connect a coming-of-age novel with other, broader ideas.

What does it mean to be feminine? A question every female asks herself at some point in her life.

Being pretty, being a mystery for men to uncover and fall in love with, being weaker yet stronger by having the manipulative power of emotion? Being clever? Using your intuition to explain the occurrences life throws at you? Typically, yes.

But if every woman abided by this feminine criteria, our lives would be monotonous and we would all be bound for the same experiences. Perhaps then, being feminine means going through life by inertia instead of a set of stereotypes/rules. To be natural and not concern yourself with what an "typical" or "exemplary" woman to do in a given situation. To not label yourself (sensitive, prideful, unforgiving, etc) because you will find yourself going against your true spirit to fulfill these qualities. Simply, to be yourself.

* * *

11.02.12

What sets apart The Perks of Being a Wallflower from other books is the protagonist's truthful, forthright analysis of what happens around him. Charlie is genuinely insightful, always generating explanations to why people act way they do.

To be victim of Charlie's sister's stingy remarks is flattering because boys are infatuated with her beauty. Her boyfriend is not an exception until she shames him publicly about a bully he was unable to confront, driving his patience to an end. This humiliating accusation spurs true confrontation: in rage, he hits her for trying to crush his dignity. To everyone's surprise, she accepts the abuse as a response to her insults because she is ultimately his bully. That is when Charlie states: ***"We accept the love we think we deserve."***

* * *

11.11.12

That simple. All the talk about social inequality, about male dominance in relationships explained in seven simple words. No need for endless essays or recurrent conventions to realize why so many women like Charlie's sister accept the tough love. One insightful teenager has summarized a message that adult feminists devoted years to propagate: there is a female factor to every situation -- not necessarily fear of or dependence on the male. The reason could be the woman's self-esteem. The way she views herself determines the people she associates with as well as the kind of treatment she expects from them. The same could be said for women who remain in dismal marriages for financial purposes. Perhaps they prioritize financial security over genuine feelings of love and respect. In that case, they're not so miserable: they simply accept the love they think they deserve. This love, however, is not for a human being but for a comfortable life, free of emotion. Feminists would argue that these women have no choice, they must live in loveless households because they are dependent on their husbands..without them they simply won't survive..it's all society's fault, etc.

In my opinion, feminism degrades a woman's potential, disregarding the role a female plays in the circumstances that affect her life. It's not always entirely the male's fault because the female has control of her life too. She may not have the greatest power in society, nevertheless she is able to establish the kind of treatment she will and will not tolerate towards herself.Charlie's sister recognized she was being repulsive towards her boyfriend and was able to forgive his abusive behavior, as shocking and "unethical" as it was. She tolerated the abuse because she believed she deserved it and even though she could have terminated the relationship, she decided to remain with her boyfriend whom she had grown to love more than ever after the incident. The irony.

~This post is definitely subject to lots of debate: I would love to hear why you agree or, even better disagree with my opinions.

Figure 3.1   Student's Reading Journal from Rebekah's Class Wiki

the wiki. While each student had an individual page to share his or her thoughts, the entries were largely composed as traditional reading responses. Rebekah did not ask students to include hyperlinks, images, or other media elements. In fact, most of Rebekah's students used only alphabetic text in this web-based writing.

In *Crafting Digital Writing*, Troy defines "web-based texts" as "more than just alphabetic text," because they contain "some form of interactive media beyond hyperlinks" (2013, p. 30). The elements that transform a text from a traditional piece of writing that simply appears on-screen to a piece of digital writing combine to create an overall effect for the reader. The whole is, indeed, more than the sum of the parts. However, Rebekah concludes that her students "were just publishing online, not crafting digital writing."

We think this distinction is important as we examine the types of digital arguments that students might read and write. Digital arguments are not just the transposition of alphabetic text onto a screen. Given the many opportunities that students have to use and consume interactive media—especially when thinking about the components described in Chapter 2—the choices that a digital writer makes when crafting a web-based argument must be judicious and strategic. Just because a writer *can* include a hyperlink, animated GIF, embedded video, or some other feature to enhance the reader's experience does not necessarily mean that the writer *should* include these elements. However, given the opportunity to do so with a web-based text, it makes sense that a writer would.

In other words, as we think about how to help digital writers construct claims and support them with evidence as well as read these kinds of arguments, we must carefully consider how each of these digital craft elements contributes to the overall effect. Does a hyperlink to a page on *Wikipedia* or a definition from Dictionary.com give the reader useful context? Or is it merely distracting? Similarly, does an image embedded from a professional photographer show details that words alone cannot, thus enhancing the overall argument, or does it divert the reader from the writing?

Thus, our goal in this chapter is to explore the kinds of knowledge that Alexandra would need in order to create robust arguments that take advantage of the technologies available when composing web-based texts. Here—as well as in Chapters 4 (infographics), 5 (videos), and 6 (social media)—we will explore different media that digital writers might employ through a series of questions that center on argument.

In each chapter we will ask and answer the following questions:

- The characteristics and content: What does this type of digital argument look like in practice? What constitutes a claim, evidence, warrant, and attention to rebuttal in this form of argument?

- The craft of composing: What does a student need to know and be able to do in order to read and write this form of digital argument?

- And, finally, a practical matter: How does a writer attend to issues of citation, plagiarism, and fair use when crafting this type of argument?

A focus on both the reading and the writing of digital texts is embedded in each chapter. We do not separate them cleanly because the connection between reading and writing, which has always been present, is increasingly powerful in an era where readers can immediately write in response to texts. Thus, we encourage you to remix and reconsider the mantra that many of us know so well: "read like a writer, write for a reader" can now become "read digital texts like a digital writer; compose digital text for an engaged reader who expects novelty and creativity."

Additionally, each chapter ends with a series of questions and key ideas with "Taking It to the Classroom." Provided as both a summary and a way to further your thinking, these final thoughts reiterate the many decisions you will need to make related to teaching declarative and procedural knowledge of form and substance. Moreover, when considering the inquiry cube we presented in Chapter 1, these lists will help you think critically about how technology can enhance the reading and writing of digital arguments.

While this chapter mainly looks at affordances of many kinds of web-based texts—including the ability to embed media, create hyperlinks, and provide comments—we will focus not on wiki pages, websites, or collaborative word-processing documents. Instead, we will examine the increasingly popular format of the blog. From students' individual blogs to classroom, school, or cross-school collaborations, blogs are a unique medium that allows students to express themselves through alphabetic text as well as images, audio, and video. For the most part, this section will zero in on the affordances of text and how the technical features of blogs can be used to craft effective digital arguments, though it is worth noting that many of these techniques can transfer to other forms of web-based text, too.

Characteristics and Content: What Do Blog Posts Look Like?

A blog is defined by *Wikipedia* as a "site published on the World Wide Web and consisting of discrete entries ('posts') typically displayed in reverse chronological order (the most recent post appears first)." These individual posts could consist of just a single word or image, or they could stretch out to hundreds of words and include various forms of media, such as embedded images and videos. Like most web-based texts, blogs feature WYSIWYG ("what you see is what you get") editors that allow for a variety of fonts, layouts, colors, and features such as bulleted lists and block quotes. Individual posts can also include tags or categories that build over time and can be represented on the blog as searchable or clickable terms that a reader can use for navigation.

The blog as a whole often includes an archive of past posts as well as individual pages. Pages differ from posts in that they usually hold a permanent place in the blog's architecture, often appearing on a menu bar. Pages may include "About," "Contact," or any other category related to the author and the general topic of the blog itself. As new posts are published to the blog, an RSS feed is automatically generated. RSS ("really simple syndication" or "rich site summary") allows the blog to "push" content to other websites and applications. One common use of RSS occurs when individuals set up an RSS reader—such as Feedly or Feedspot—to keep track of multiple websites and their newest posts.

In thinking about the ways we might share this information about blogs with students, one possibility would be to present this list of features (Table 3.1) in a minilesson, then analyze some mentor texts to identify those features. What is a blog post? What does it look like? What is the content? This is the declarative knowledge that our students need, and in order to understand some of these concepts, they need a working knowledge of technology. And, we hope, after learning this information, our students would likely do well on a quiz about what blogs are and how they work.

However, this type of declarative knowledge is not enough for digital writers to be successful. We also want them to be able to use procedural knowledge in order

Table 3.1 Characteristics and Content of Blog Posts

Characteristics of a Blog Post (Declarative Knowledge of Form)	Content of a Blog Post (Declarative Knowledge of Substance)
• Contains roughly 250–1,000 words; longer than a social network update and shorter than a typical magazine or newspaper feature article • Usually employs a first-person point of view • Includes links to outside resources including news items, other blog posts, or various media • Develops with short paragraphs that are aesthetically pleasing and functional for reading • Utilizes additional text features such as images, subheadings, and bulleted lists • Allows for commentary from readers • Provides a permalink, author's name, and timestamp, with posts usually presented in reverse chronological order	• Reflects the general focus of the blog but, as one entry in an entire blog's history, a post explores a particular issue, concept, or question • Draws on personal anecdotes and experiences, as well as statistics and other forms of evidence • Speaks to a public audience as part of a networked conversation, including links to other blogs, thus joining a larger conversation about a particular topic or issue • Presents ideas in an informational or argumentative mode, with the general expectation that the content will include facts as well as interpretive analysis and opinion (usually not written as fiction)

to craft effective digital arguments. In this case, we wonder how Rebekah might be able to help her students move from simply posting their reading responses online to creating a more nuanced, complex argument that would involve the use of hyperlinks, images, or other media as a critical part of their overall argument. It is this type of procedural knowledge that we will explore throughout the rest of this chapter, examining samples from both a professional blogger and another high school student.

What Constitutes a Claim, Evidence, Warrant, and Attention to Rebuttal in a Blog Post?

Scott McLeod is a prominent edublogger (http://dangerouslyirrelevant.org/) whose posts range from short informational announcements to longer argumentative pieces. His blog dates back to August of 2006, and he writes on a variety of topics related to education, leadership, and twenty-first-century learning. Figure 3.2 presents one post, "Why Would Students Feel Valued at School?," which we will deconstruct with a Toulmin analysis to see exactly how McLeod uses the media available to him to present evidence and make a claim.

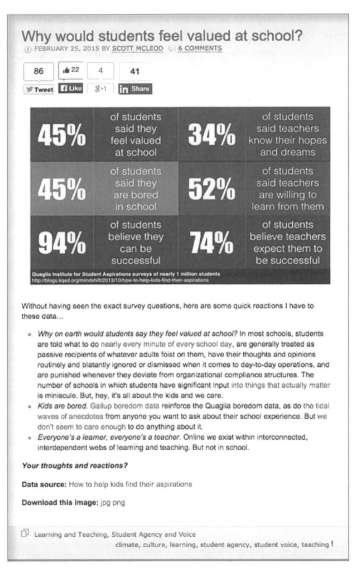

Figure 3.2 Post by Scott McLeod: "Why Would Students Feel Valued at School?"

McLeod opens with statistics in graphic form. He uses an image—one that he created specifically for this blog post, as compared to listing the statistics—because it draws the reader to the evidence he is presenting simply by the size, shape, and color of the graphic. He explores his "reactions to this data" in a bulleted list, incorporating several links (outlined in Table 3.2). He concludes with an invitation to conversation from his readers: "Your thoughts and reactions?"

McLeod makes compositional choices that align with the general modes of blogging that are made possible by the media. If we compare the post to the features of a blog that we outlined in Table 3.1, we can check off every point.

But what is the specific content of this post? What argument is he making? And even more important, how does McLeod use the media to craft an argument? Let's break down the three bullet points in his post by doing a Toulmin analysis.

Table 3.2 Links in McLeod's Post

Text from McLeod's Post	Summary of Destination Link
nearly every minute of every school day	Another of his posts where he provides a warrant that says schools are not set up to help kids "make a dent in the universe"
into things that actually matter	Another of his posts where he makes an argument about giving students "real voice"
Gallup data	An opinion piece by the executive director of Gallup that cites statistics
tidal wave of anecdotes	Does not link to a story but to a quote from *The Game of School* that summarizes our own experience (expert opinion)
we don't seem to care enough	Another quote from *The Game of School*
How to help kids find their aspirations	The KQED article that, in essence, makes the claim: "To do that, Quaglia suggests focusing on three guiding principles: self-worth, engagement, and purpose. Helping students work on these qualities will ultimately help them to feel academic motivation, a clear predictor of academic achievement."

Bullet 1

Claim:　We should not expect students to say they feel valued at school.

Evidence:　"In most schools, students are told what to do <u>nearly every minute of every school day</u>, are generally treated as passive recipients of whatever adults foist on them, have their thoughts and opinions routinely and blatantly ignored or dismissed when it comes to day-to-day operations, and are punished whenever they deviate from organizational compliance structures. The number of schools in which students have significant input into things that actually matter is miniscule."

Warrant: A person who is given no authority or opinion with regard to decision making will likely not feel valued. (implied)

Bullet 2

Claim: Kids are bored.

Evidence: Quaglia Institute boredom data. (in the graphic)

Gallup boredom data. (link to article)

Warrant: The self-reports from the kids, as presented by these reputable organizations, are embedded in a context described in the quotes from Robert Fried's *The Game of School* (2005), making the claim valid. (implied with stated context)

Bullet 3

Claim: In school not everyone is a learner and a teacher.

Evidence: Fifty-two percent of students said teachers are willing to learn from them.

Warrant: If nearly half of students do not feel that teachers are willing to learn from them, then not everyone in the school is a learner and a teacher. (implied)

McLeod does not present his argument in a way that makes this analysis easy. In fact, we struggled to identify his primary claim in the post. Given the links he provides to *The Game of School*, which provide context for warranting the evidence he presents, we think the three subclaims outlined in the bullets speak to a larger implicit claim: We do not care enough about kids to give them authority and make them feel valued. Uncovering this implied claim requires deep reading of the digital text.

In school we teach students to write claims clearly in each argument that they make. However, as a skilled writer and reputable blogger, McLeod does not make this move; because he has written about this issue before, he links to his previously published thoughts, allowing his readers to deduce (and perhaps even to shape through comments) his overall argument. This requires the reader to understand the broader context of McLeod's work and read closely to infer his various meanings.

As a skilled digital writer, McLeod uses images and hyperlinks to provide and warrant the evidence for his claims. At some points he cites himself, and at others he relies on outside sources. As his post also demonstrates, a link can easily substitute for a traditional in-text citation. All of these rhetorical choices—implied claims and warrants with explicit evidence, presenting information in text as well as graphic form, and citing his sources—support his argument.

As noted earlier, blogging occurs within a larger set of conversations that have been occurring over time. Using hyperlinks allows a blogger to connect, quite literally, to other people and points in that conversation. For this reason, claims might be implicit because they have been made before. Readers and writers of blogs must understand this networked context as they navigate digital arguments. Of course, if we were curious, we could ask McLeod in the comments section of the blog, responding to his invitation to join the conversation. He invites our questions, our thoughts, and even our rebuttals in his invitation to comment, to leave a voice recording, or to connect with him via email or social networks. This extended conversation, as Toulmin might say, is what makes an argument, and the medium of blog allows for his continued attention to rebuttal.

The Craft of Composing: What Does a Student Need to Know and Be Able to Do to Read and Write a Blog Post?

Using professional blog posts as mentor texts allows for conversations about what constitutes various aspects of argument in this medium. Naming the features of a blog post represents the declarative knowledge that students will need in order to craft this form of argument; if we want our students to produce a blog post, we need to engage them in the practices bloggers use. Our work here, then, is to shift from declarative to procedural knowledge.

To further explore this aspect of blogging, we now turn to Khadi, a student writer from Norway who blogs at https://perfectionitself.wordpress.com. In her post from March 2015 (shown in Figure 3.3), "Controversial Statements and the General Election," Khadi argues that a minor political party, UKIP, "is laden with problematic statements and a subject of much loathing, [yet] it does have supporters and is growing year by year" (Daudova 2015).

CONTROVERSIAL STATEMENTS AND THE GENERAL ELECTION

Yesterday: Ban the jobless from driving to ease congestion, Ukip candidate says. Obviously this is a controversial statement. Not very surprising, though. Ukip representatives manage to utter these kind of statements seemingly every day. Who can forget Kerry Smith's leaked phone calls and Ukip leader's Nigel Farage wish to join forces with Russia. Believe me; there are plenty of those.

On 7th of May, the United Kingdom is having their general election. Now, Ukip is not a big party (they only have two seats), but they did win the fourth most votes during the 2010 election and it is predicted that their seat gain is almost guaranteed. The real competition is between the Conservatives, the largest single party currently in coalition with the Liberal Democrats, and the Labours. 303 and 257 are their current seats in the House of Commons. However, we can't ignore the fact that Ukip placed first in the 2014 European Elections.

While Ukip is laden with problematic statements and a subject of much loathing, it does have supporters and is growing year by year.

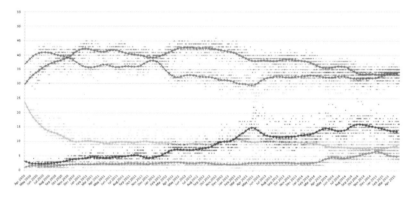

This chart shows opinion polling for the general election from 2010 to the predictions in the future. The purple line represents Ukip. It variates through the months, but the rise of the party is quite clear. Maybe in some years from now Ukip will be a substantial competitor to the Conservatives and the Labours? In my case, I hope not.

Sources

Ban the jobless from driving to ease congestion, Ukip candidate says

Farage's golden boy's rant at 'pooftahs', 'Chigwell Peasants' and 'Chinky bird': Astonishing leaked phone calls expose outbursts of Ukip man sent in to replace Neil Hamilton

Nigel Farage: Stop opposing Vladmir Putin in Ukraine and join forces to defeat Islamic terrorists

European Elections: UKIP Tops British Polls

Figure 3.3 Post from Khadi's Blog

Her first paragraph presents evidence, by way of links to three articles from the UK's *Telegraph* and *Daily Mail*, highlighting the controversial and problematic statements made by party leaders. Khadi even explicitly states a warrant: "Obviously, this is a controversial statement." This sentence, though simple and direct, clearly ties the evidence to her claim. At the end of the paragraph, she addresses a potential audience (and perhaps a rebuttal) by saying, "Believe me, there are plenty of those [examples]."

Her second paragraph presents evidence, in the form of both alphabetic text (e.g., "UKIP placed first in the 2014 elections") and image. She includes a graph that shows several years of opinion polling, again warranting this evidence explicitly with the statement that "the rise of the party is quite clear." Finally, she provides a list of linked sources at the end of her post.

As we assess Khadi's writing, we see that she knows, procedurally, how to craft an argument:

- She makes a claim that is easy to understand.

- She uses evidence from a variety of credible news sources, included both as hyperlinks and in a list of sources at the end.

- She offers statements that serve to warrant her evidence.

- She acknowledges readers (and possible other viewpoints) with direct address and a conversational tone.

In examining Khadi's procedural knowledge of crafting arguments in a blog post, we also see that she knows how to insert hyperlinks as a form of evidence (both in the writing itself, as a form of in-text citation, and in a list of sources) as well as an image that serves as evidence. As a high school student and beginning blogger, Khadi has begun to develop procedural knowledge of digital writing. While we were fortunate enough to find Khadi's blog, we have not worked with her directly. If one of us were her writing teacher, however, after working further with Khadi and her classmates, we might design lessons on categorizing and tagging her post, linking to other articles that extend the conversation, and inviting reader response to her argument. We would compliment her on her use of the graphic and encourage her to cite the source directly (as Scott McLeod does below his image).

Khadi's post is but one example among thousands of posts that students around the world make each day. While many of these writers use solely alphabetic text to make arguments (like Alexandra's reading log in Figure 3.1), others, like Khadi, attend to features of blogging—specifically the use of hyperlinks, embedded media, and a strong stance as a writer—to craft digitally. As teachers, we want to see where our students are writing and help them to engage fully as digital writers by applying their declarative and procedural knowledge.

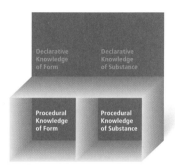

We strongly believe that it is not enough to have students do what they normally do on paper (or even with a word processing program) and publish it online. Instead, we need to teach them to craft an argument using media in strategic ways. In Table 3.3, which correlates to the declarative knowledge of form and substance discussed in the previous section, we articulate the strategies of production that we would teach in order to develop procedural knowledge of composing blog posts.

As Smith et al. state, "The development of declarative and procedural knowledge are intimately related" (2012, p. 24). So too, we feel, are the development of procedural knowledge of substance and form when we consider the use of tools of technology. It is not just about how a writer inserts a link, but how she chooses to insert a link on a particular word or phrase that helps the reader to understand the argument being made. In this case, for example, generating links and using links to advance the argument straddle both categories. When it comes to teaching students how to write effective digital arguments, we think it's okay to be torn about whether adding a link might be best categorized as procedural knowledge of form or procedural knowledge of substance. What's important is that students develop an understanding of what the form looks like, as well as an ability to produce the various features of the form. These production strategies increasingly call for knowledge of technology that will ultimately help them to craft effective digital arguments.

Practical Matters: How Does a Writer Attend to Issues of Citation, Plagiarism, and Fair Use When Crafting Web-Based Text?

Composing an argument with web-based text offers writers some unique opportunities. Most notably, as demonstrated in both the professional and student examples in this chapter, digital writers can embed hyperlinks and media that can help provide evidence for their claim. For instance, rather than having to write out a typical sen-

Table 3.3 The Craft of Blog Posts

Craft Element	Ability to Create a Blog Post (Procedural Knowledge of Form) To produce the features of a blog post as a particular mode of writing, how do you . . .	Ability to Find and Generate Content for a Blog Post (Procedural Knowledge of Substance) To produce the content of an individual blog post, how do you . . .
Hyperlinks	• Create a hyperlink from your blog post to other content available on the Internet?	• Choose exactly what content the link connects to, whether internal or external? • Choose the words that will become a hyperlink? • Use links strategically to advance the argument you are making?
Conciseness	• Write short, focused paragraphs that accentuate main ideas and may include bulleted lists of key points?	• Identify a focus? • Articulate a claim? • Use evidence to support a claim through statements, bullets, links, or multimedia? • Warrant that evidence implicitly or explicitly, through statements or links? • Generate the content of the post?
Media	• Embed images, video, or other multimedia?	• Choose existing images, videos, or multimedia content? • Acknowledge sources and respect copyright, fair use, or other forms of content licensing? • Align your media within the text of the blog post for maximum effect?
Web-based features	• Use an HTML editor to publish a post and distribute the link via social networks? • Respond to comments left on your blog post as well as provide comments to other bloggers writing about a similar topic?	• Identify the network for sharing? • Decide the type of response needed (e.g., claim, evidence, warrant, backing) and generate that content?

tence that would include markers for an upcoming citation ("In their article, Jones and Smith claim that _____"), a blogger can include a hyperlink to the source, whether it is an academic article, a story on popular media, a personal blog, a *Wikipedia* page, or anything else online. Additionally, digital writers can embed other media into their own web-based texts, most notably images and video.

These options raise important questions about citation, plagiarism, and fair use. In this section, which appears in Chapters 3 through 6, we will offer a few insights and related questions about these issues. Because this is the first time we are providing background on our thinking, we should let you know that both of us have taken a stance on copyright and fair use by reading and viewing materials created by media scholar Renee Hobbs. Her 2010 book *Copyright Clarity: How Fair Use Supports Digital Learning* (along with its partner website, http://mediaeducationlab.com/copyright) offers a variety of resources on these issues, and we strongly recommend that you review her work.

For the moment, we must summarize some of her big ideas. In short, one of the key ideas that we have learned from studying Hobbs' work is that citation and plagiarism concern academic ethics, whereas copyright and fair use concern laws. This may seem like a subtle difference, but this difference matters. Using copyrighted materials and avoiding plagiarism are overlapping and interrelated, especially when thinking about how to have our students find, manage, and cite sources that include text, images, video, and other forms of media. We need to consider how we can have students employ the principles of fair use so they can repurpose copyrighted material, doing so in a transformative manner, and at the same time honor the academic tradition of citing one's sources. In this sense, we rely on the definition of "transformative" that Hobbs provides in *Copyright Clarity*. She frames "transformativeness" as a question: "Does the new work merely supersede the objects of the original creation, or instead does it add something new, with a further purpose or different character, altering the first with new expression, meaning, or message?" (p. 44).

In Khadi's blog post, for instance, we see the issue of citation and fair use come to a head when she includes the chart from another source. From a copyright perspective, Hobbs argues that, "fair use gives people a right to use copyrighted material when the cost to the copyright holder is less than the social benefit of the use of the copyrighted work" (p. 19). There are no hard and fast rules that can assure a student or teacher that he or she is using copyrighted material appropriately. Instead, Hobbs continues, "[t]o determine if fair use applies, individuals must assess the specific context and situation concerning the use of a copyrighted work" (p. 19).

Again, we point to another of Hobbs' resources, a thinking guide that scaffolds the fair use reasoning process (http://copyrightconfusion.wikispaces.com /Reasoning). Using the questions in the guide, both Kristen and Troy agree that Khadi used the image rightfully under the provisions of fair use. We believe this for a few reasons, based on the "four pillars" of fair use:

- What is the type of use? Khadi is using an image from another source as a way to augment her own argument in an academic blog post. She is not trying to attract clicks on another news site and generate advertising dollars.

- What is the nature of the material? Khadi is using the graph, created by someone else, to highlight the growth of the UKIP Party. She has taken an image that, in this case, she most likely would not be able to replicate on her own (at least not without hours and hours of work).

- How much of the original copyrighted material is she using? This answer, unfortunately, is a bit harder to discern in Khadi's case. Because we don't know the original source (and thus whether the graph was part of a longer article or stood alone), we don't know how much original material she is using. Still, we are guessing that it is one part of a larger article.

- What is the effect on the market for the original material? In this case, it is very unlikely that Khadi's blog will attract more readers than the original article, pulling traffic (and advertising dollars) from that website.

So, under these conditions, we agree that Khadi is using the original copyrighted material fairly. However, Khadi's use of this particular image raises a different concern about citation. While she was conscious of linking to other sources, both in the text itself and in a list of resources at the end, neither of us could find this graph on the web pages she linked to. As noted above, this is one of the concerns that we would have about her ability to translate declarative knowledge of blogging (many bloggers use images to support their ideas) and the technical features that blogs afford (how to embed an image) into the procedural knowledge that she needs as an academic writer. In short, academic writing requires that you cite your sources. While it is true that she had the right to include the image under the rules of fair use, she should also clearly indicate where the image originated with an accurate citation or link.

Because this is such a complex issue, and because Khadi's is but one example, we summarize our conversation about copyright and citation for this chapter by reminding teachers: no student ever found an article or an image "on Google" (or Yahoo, Bing, or any other search engine). The search engine is merely the tool that people use to find articles and images that are created by others and hosted on their respective web servers. We should be helping students—even those in elementary school—to understand that everything on the Internet has a "home" in the sense that it is hosted on a domain and was put there by someone else. All items online have a URL and can therefore be cited. Being able to find and use copyrighted material through a web search is just one step in the process; being able to cite the material properly is a critical digital writing skill.

Taking It to the Classroom

In thinking, then, about the ways that affordances of web-based texts can be used to craft an effective argument, we must be mindful of numerous factors, including the quality of the writing itself as well as the media elements allowed through the web-based platform, such as links, images, and videos. First, as we have always done when teaching argument writing, we must have students use clear reasoning and effective evidence to support their claims. Second, we want them to be especially mindful of how, when, and why they include these elements so that they are not superfluous and ultimately support the argument in smart ways.

The following are key ideas and questions to consider:

- Digital texts have technical elements (hyperlinks, embedded media, text and features such as images, subheadings, bulleted lists) that can also be employed as rhetorical elements. How can students use these elements to get their readers' attention and support their arguments with evidence?

- Digital texts offer opportunities for readers to comment and can be circulated to wide audiences. In what ways can students invite their readers into a broader conversation by including links to relevant sources and posing questions that spark conversation?

- Although digital texts open up opportunities for students to cite and use the work of others—including quotes, pictures, charts, videos, and other media—they also raise questions about plagiarism and copyright. How can you engage students in conversations about fair use and citation during the digital reading and writing process?

Thus, many questions remain, even after a thorough exploration of digital texts. In many ways, this feels disheartening because there is no one "right" way to answer any of these questions, even with the heuristics we have shared. However, we encourage you—and your students—to keep thinking about the questions that will, in turn, make them stronger as digital readers and writers. Here are a few ways that you can bring the study of web-based texts into your classroom:

- Invite students to identify two web-based stories about the same topic, but from different sources. Ask them to categorize the links, noting where the links lead and for what purposes. Are the links similar? Do they differ widely? Why do you think that is?

- Allow students to critique the arguments made by bloggers, news reporters, and website authors. Have them articulate the claims being made. Are they clearly stated? Should they be? What kind of evidence do the authors provide? Do the links support the claims? Is the evidence clearly linked? Does the reader get lost "down the rabbit hole" with too many links?

- Ask your students to blog about many of the things you are reading in class, with attention to the craft of digital argument. When asking them to explain something, suggest they include a relevant hyperlink or embedded example. Ask them to reflect on how the hyperlinked material supports, counters, or extends their argument.

With tasks and lessons like these to support writers, students like Alexandra and Khadi will be better able to critically read and write digital arguments with web-based texts. Next we will turn our attention to a visual medium: infographics.

CHAPTER 4

THE MOVES OF ARGUMENT IN INFOGRAPHICS

Allison Marchetti (@AllisonMarchett), coauthor of *Writing with Mentors* and blogger at MovingWriters.org, asks her students to create infographics as a form of argument. She began by creating a board of infographics on Learnist, a site that describes itself as "a place for learning and sharing what you know" to act as mentor texts for her students. Then, she asked them to study this collection by jotting notes as they read and viewed them, focusing on three questions:

- What do you notice?

- What do these texts have in common?

- According to these examples, what is an infographic? What are the features of an infographic?

Together, they developed their own definitions, which we will return to later in the chapter. For the moment, we can rely on *Wikipedia*'s description of infographics: "graphic visual representations of information, data or knowledge intended to present complex information quickly and clearly." Infographics have become an increasingly popular means of expressing information and making arguments. Perhaps because of their visual appeal, perhaps because they are so easy to "like," "retweet," or "pin," infographics are a steady part of the content readers consume online.

The first documented infographic was published in 1869, with Charles Minard's skillful outline of Napoleon's march upon Russia, as well as his ultimate defeat, in the "Figurative Map of the Successive Losses in Men of the French Army in the Russian Campaign 1812–1813."

Tracing the rise of visual arguments through the twentieth century, scholar Edward Tufte notes in *The Visual Display of Quantitative Information* (1983, p. 191): "What is to be sought in designs for the display of information is the clear portrayal of complexity. Not the complication of the simple; rather the task of the designer is to give visual access to the subtle and the difficult—that is, revelation of the complex."

Until recently, this ability to "reveal the complex" through the design of infographics required sophisticated knowledge of both mathematics and design principles. And, while our students still need numeracy skills and a sharp, well-trained eye, web-based tools such as Piktochart, Infogram, and Easel.ly make it easier than ever before for authors to combine images, text, links, charts, and graphs to create infographics that can easily be shared, bringing digital readers and writers together in conversation.

For instance, RJ Andrews, blogger of *In Info We Trust*, composed the "Creative Routines" infographic, which compares the work routines of productive "composers, painters, writers, scientists, philosophers." Using a clockface as the central organizing theme, he represents sleep, work, exercise, eating, and other areas of these individuals' lives through color coding. The original post from March 26, 2014, had, at the time of this writing, 271 replies in the comments, and has been shared hundreds of times on social media. Rather than seeing the information as simply data, commenters quickly absorbed the information and began drawing comparisons to their own lives. This is just one example of how a digital writer has taken a variety of media elements—facts in the form of written text, photographs, colors, fonts, shapes, and intelligent use of white space—to generate compelling digital writing that can be consumed and comprehended in just one glance and invite a variety of responses from readers.

Though Andrews integrated quite a bit of data in his infographic, we know that some designers also use the medium to oversimplify or slant information to support a particular view or claim; thus, understanding the design features of infographics can help students to read deeply and uncover bias. In addition, because infographics present data—numerical, written, and visual—they can be a powerful medium for making arguments, and we think they are a mode worth teaching.

Characteristics and Content: What Do Infographics Look Like?

At their core, infographics are a combination of words, numbers, and visual elements. Yet this description oversimplifies the way that writers think about composing this type of digital text. In reviewing a number of examples as well as articles about what constitutes effective infographics, a few key themes stood out to us.

First, the data presented must have a compelling "story." Many of the resources we reviewed refer to "story" in the sense of marketing and brand development, not in the sense of having a narrator, or rising action, or a protagonist and antagonist. Bernadette Jiwa, on her website Brand Story, describes the story as "a complete picture made up of facts, feelings and interpretations" about a brand. Or, as Valentine Belonwu notes in "The Absolutely Essential Components of an Eye-Catching, Informative Infographic": "[Y]ou have to be able to tell a story combing [sic] both the data and graphics. By putting it all together in a format that is easy to read and understand, you will draw your audience in and keep them hooked."

Second, the data must be attributed to a reliable source. Designer Gurjot Bhuller explains:

> *The most important component of an infographic is accurate data . . . As an organization, you may already have data you can use, you just need to find it and sort it. Wherever the data comes from, you need to make sure it is credited somewhere on the infographic. Uncredited information is not only unethical, but is untrustworthy to most readers.*

Finally, the infographic needs to be aesthetically pleasing and, from a technical sense, easy to distribute. On her *Socially Sorted* blog, Donna Moritz describes both the visual and the technical elements that improve an infographic's "shareability." These include a web post in which the original graphic is shared; proper social media plug-ins for easy tweeting, pinning, and liking; and embedded code that allows others to use the infographic easily.

With these professional views on the mode of infographic in mind, we return to some of the definitions offered by Allison's students, generated across three class periods through a whole-class discussion and captured in a Google Doc (see Table 4.1).

Table 4.1 Definitions of Infographics from Allison's Students

Notes from first-period class:	Notes from second-period class:	Notes from third-period class:
What is an infographic?		
A visual image that contains easy-to-understand charts and graphs, in addition to creative colors and graphics, to help communicate a thesis, argument, or "so what"	Any static visual presentation that creatively incorporates the use of words, statistics, and images in order to convey a message	A combination of information and graphics (colorful pictures, images, and graphs) that give reasons and ideas to back up a thesis on a topic
What makes an infographic an infographic?		
• Charts and graphs illustrating a topic through details, stats, and data • Eye-catching • Color palette helps reinforce the message • Pictures with short descriptive bits • Introductory blurb to explain purpose behind infographic • References/works cited • The "composer" uses colors and fonts to bring attention to important point	• Infographics show more than tell • Infographics cite their sources in different ways (at bottom of page and also throughout the infographic) • Infographics break down one main topic and supply "bits" of information throughout • LAYOUT—one that flows, color scheme, font (size and style) • Information in the form of statistics, comparisons, charts (pie, bar, table, etc.), diagrams, and graphics	• They "show" rather than tell about a topic/argument • They "show" with numbers, statistics, and data to make what they are trying to argue true and factual • Often IGs try to present information in a way that lets the reader deduce or infer an argument/idea • Utilize different types of charts: bar, pie, line, and/or graphics, timelines, and visual aids • Do the thinking for the reader, presenting conclusions in a kind of list • Layout helps build the argument: font, colors, layout • Stronger IGs have fewer words—no paragraphs, but "bits"

We think Allison's students have done a pretty good job articulating the features of an infographic, and we've taken their work, alongside our own research, to help us complete our declarative knowledge chart in Table 4.2.

Table 4.2 Characteristics and Content of Infographics

Conventional Characteristics of an Infographic (Declarative Knowledge of Form)	**Content of an Infographic** (Declarative Knowledge of Substance)
<ul><li>Statistics presented in numerical form or as a chart</li><li>Art (ranging from clip art to highly designed art specific to the work)</li><li>Directional signals (arrows, line breaks)</li><li>Shapes (which may represent relationships or motion)</li><li>Recurring patterns, fonts, and colors, as well as appropriate use of white space (Williams' CRAP principles; see page 40)</li><li>Provides a legend if needed</li><li>A (relatively) clear "path" through the infographic (typical left-to-right, top-to-bottom reading may not apply)</li><li>Clearly identifies the topic with headline, images, and overall design</li><li>Short segments of text; generally, few words or a sentence limited to explaining the statistics at hand (caption-like), though one infographic may have many of these segments</li><li>Includes links to additional sources, references to add credibility</li><li>Identifies the graphic's author/illustrator</li></ul>	<ul><li>Tells a story</li><li>Makes a clear claim, though it may be implicit</li><li>Presents reliable and useful data that connects to the claim</li><li>May offer rebuttal to a counterargument but often slants toward one side</li></ul>

What Constitutes a Claim, Evidence, Warrant, and Attention to Rebuttal in an Infographic?

Infographics are generally considered to be one-sided arguments that discount or ignore other perspectives. They present claims, yet those claims may be implied rather than explicit. Based on our experience with more traditional, print-based texts, we might expect the claim to be obvious in the headline/title or subheadings. However, infographics can also use graphic elements to imply claims, using color, scale, layout, and design to present ideas in a favorable or unfavorable light, to emphasize or downplay information, or to invoke particular reactions from an audience.

Furthermore, because effective infographics rely on a tightly focused message, they rarely present an alternative perspective, let alone a fully formed counterargument. Readers must be savvy enough to know to check additional sources to determine accuracy.

For instance, in the infographic in Figure 4.1, we see a number of these traits that social media experts—and Allison's students—identified as important. This particular infographic comes from the website JustStand.org, whose mission is, in part, to raise "awareness about the dangers of excessive sitting" and to collaborate "with researchers and supporting studies to further our understanding of sedentary behavior and its antidotes." Digging just a little deeper, we find out that this website is produced by Ergotron, a company that sells standing desks, monitor wall mounts, and other modern

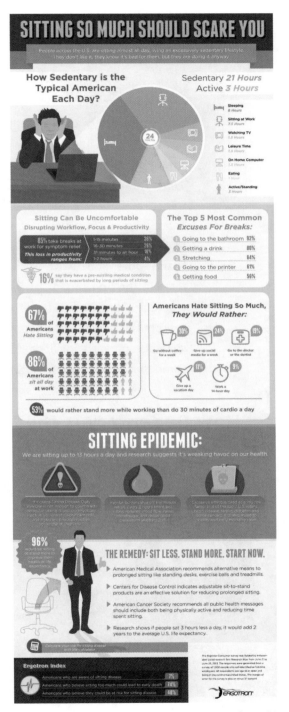

Figure 4.1 "Sitting So Much Should Scare You" Infographic

ergonomic devices. They note that this website represents a shared effort where "like-minded academic leaders and business groups began collaborating on projects to improve our work environments."

Thus, when we first look at Figure 4.1, "Sitting So Much Should Scare You," a critical reader will already be taking these potential biases or conflicts of interest into account. On the infographic itself, Ergotron notes that it conducted a four-day survey of "1,000 people who self identified as full-time employees"; it also draws on references from additional sources, including *Bloomberg*, the *New York Times*, the *Los Angeles Times*, the American Medical Association, and the American Cancer Society. The infographic is broken into roughly five subsections, and we will examine just a few pieces of evidence that are presented within the entire graphic to show how they ultimately reach their conclusion for "The Remedy: Sit Less. Stand More. Start Now."

In the first section of the infographic, pictured next to a drawing of an office worker holding his head in his hands in frustration, is a pie chart (Figure 4.2). It represents the twenty-four hours in a day and shows the representative slices of time spent sleeping, sitting at work, watching TV, enjoying leisure activities, sitting at the computer, and eating; finally, in a distinct orange color that is repeated throughout

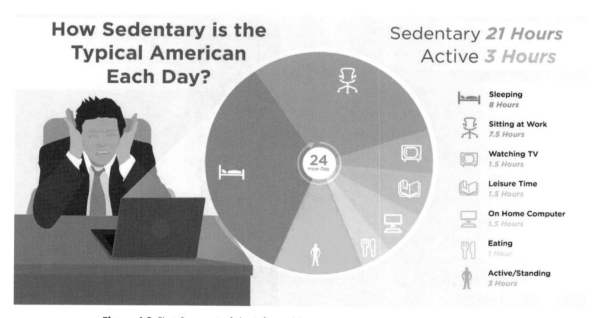

Figure 4.2 First Segment of the Infographic

the document, is the category for "active/standing." Both the color and position of this category suggest that standing or being active is our lowest priority, and that we should be alarmed.

In the next segment of the infographic (Figure 4.3), the headline suggests that "sitting can be uncomfortable" and that it can disrupt workflow, focus, and productivity. Noting that 85 percent of workers "take breaks at work for symptom relief" (from sitting), the designers then highlight the number of people who lost time as percentages. An arrow leading to the right then brings a viewer to the "top 5 most common excuses for breaks." Oddly, this evidence does not account for reasonable and customary breaks that workers are allowed, yet the point that they are trying to make is clear: sitting ultimately causes discomfort and interrupts productivity, and the arrow provides a sense of urgency.

The next segment (Figure 4.4) outlines a number of reasons why American workers hate sitting and what they would rather do instead, including such enviable options as "go without coffee for a week," "give up social media for a week," or "work a 14-hour day." As a reader, it is a little bit difficult to understand how these trade-offs are directly connected to the benefits of standing. If, for instance, someone was forced to go without coffee in order to have the option to stand, is this survey saying that 30 percent of workers would find that attractive? And, if so, what does that suggest about how much we really "hate" sitting? In short, we question the warrants that connect this data to the overall claim. At any rate, this midsection of the infographic is designed to make it clear that sitting too much is a problem about productivity as much as it is about attitude.

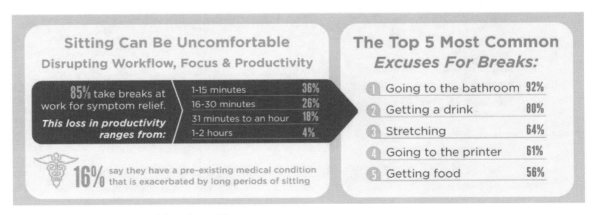

Figure 4.3 Second Segment of the Infographic

Figure 4.4 Third Segment of the Infographic

Moving into the fourth segment of the infographic (Figure 4.5), the reader is introduced to the "Sitting Epidemic," complete with a dire warning in the subhead— "We are sitting up to 13 hours a day and research suggests it's wreaking havoc on our health"—as well as graphics in the form of warning symbols such as an alert sign, big blood droplet, and a tombstone, each with a skull embedded. Along with the text beneath each graphic, the strong visual imagery that associates sitting with death makes the reader pause to consider the potential peril of a sedentary lifestyle.

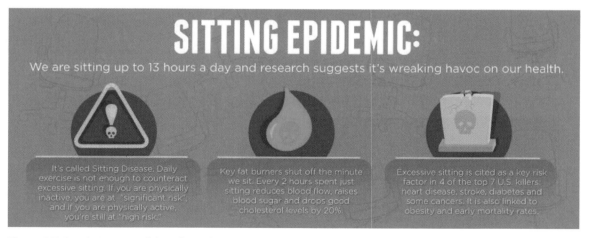

Figure 4.5 Fourth Segment of the Infographic

The visual highlights the evidence presented, serving as a warrant to the claim.

Finally, we near the end of the graphic and the conclusion to its claim about sitting: we simply need to stand more (Figure 4.6). They pound this point with a statistic from their survey—"96% would be willing to stand more to improve their health or life expectancy"—accentuated with an image of the worker standing next to his chair and an arrow visually pushing him out of it. To fully drive the point home, a list of statements about standing from the American Medical Association, Centers for Disease Control, and American Cancer Society, along with the classic phrase, "Research shows . . . ," make the case clear.

In sum, "Sitting So Much Should Scare You" is designed as a campaign to get people interested in the idea of ergonomic office furniture, specifically the kinds of products designed by Ergotron, the parent company. If you continue to sit at work, the blunt conclusion is that you will die an early death. So in one sense, it is an elaborate advertisement. Yet, to give the company credit, it is producing products that can potentially—in conjunction with other lifestyle choices—help make people healthier. Ergotron references a number of outside sources as well as its own survey results.

The infographic, as an argument, does indeed provide evidence—as well as effective visual design that in some cases clearly warrants that evidence—that standing at work could result in better health, improved attitude, and increased productivity. Of course, the ad doesn't present much of a counterargument, but you

Figure 4.6 Final Segment of the Infographic

can't blame the company for wanting to sell its furniture products. So, any student analyzing this argument would be wise to check additional sources, such as a recent report from National Public Radio's medical team, which concludes that "there isn't really any evidence that standing is better than sitting" (Chen 2016), as a way to check the claims in this infographic.

The Craft of Composing: What Does a Student Need to Know and Be Able to Do to Read and Write Infographics?

Lara Tomenchok, a student in Allison Marchetti's class, was charged with the task of creating an argument through an infographic. She created the product in Figure 4.7, "Why Is Breakfast the Most Important Meal of the Day?" If we examine Lara's work, we can assess her understanding of *how* to make this kind of argument, or her procedural knowledge.

Figure 4.7 Lara's Infographic

First, let's look at what Lara knows about the form of an infographic. This product combines images and text and attends to the elements of CRAP design (articulated in Chapter 2) to create a visually appealing piece. Lara's attention to contrast, repetition, alignment, and proximity helps the reader to establish a reading path and to synthesize information that might appear random if it were not so carefully presented.

From this standpoint, it seems that Lara has developed the knowledge of how to manipulate these various elements on the screen in a way that meets her purposes as a digital writer. Furthermore, she has embedded numerical data and linked to her references. Not only does she understand that an infographic should include these elements (declarative knowledge), she also has been able to produce them (procedural knowledge).

Table 4.3 lists the procedural knowledge of form that a student needs in order to critically consume or compose an infographic. Lara has demonstrated competence

Table 4.3 Applying Williams' CRAP Criteria to Lara's Infographic

Contrast	Repetition	Alignment	Proximity
• Contrasting colors to delineate a reading path • Contrasting column width with the biggest ideas in the wider column and supporting details ("worst to best breakfasts") in the narrower column • Contrasting font sizes on the headlines and remaining text to spotlight the most important words *(Breakfast, Best, Worst)*	• Repeated use of short sentences, statistics, lines, and graphic elements of approximately the same size • Repeated use of the concept "Percent __" with "Percent healthier," "Percent better," and "Percent less" • Repeated use of "more" and "less" with sweets, soft drinks, vegetables, and fruit	• An intentionally soft edge on the percentages and black lines between the five fact sets to help the text integrate with the photo (might a cleaner alignment have been easier for readers to navigate?) • Left alignment of text in the "worst to best breakfast" column • Center alignment of percentages in the graphic elements for sweets, soft drinks, vegetables, and fruit	• Like items are clustered together—text in percentages in the center column and text with an image in the right column • Might more neutral space between the pancake stack and the main column of text have made the text easier to read?

Table 4.4 The Craft of Infographics

Craft Element	Ability to Create an Infographic (Procedural Knowledge of Form) To produce the features of an infographic as a particular mode of writing, how do you . . .	Ability to Find and Generate Content for an Infographic (Procedural Knowledge of Substance) To produce the content of an individual infographic, how do you . . .
Story	• Insert data, media, and visual design elements in a coherent manner that guides the reader? • Compose short written text to augment the data, using phrases, sentences, brief paragraphs, bulleted lists, or footnotes?	• Identify the intended audience and desired tone? • Identify a single, clear claim? • Select data to support the claim? • Determine whether claim and warrants must be explicitly stated? • Create a visual story of the argument?

Data	• Import data and create graphs, charts, percentages, etc.?
	• Embed those numerical representations in the infographic?
		• Conduct primary research:
		  ○ Design a survey and use a form to collect data?
		  ○ Disaggregate and connect data, choosing the most compelling data from your set?
		• Access existing data:
		  ○ Conduct deep Internet searches and evaluate sources?
		  ○ Research public data sets (e.g., UN, Pew)?
		  ○ Compare results across existing data sets?
		• Determine the reliability of the data and how the audience will respond?

Media	• Insert an image such as:
	  ○ Available clip art and shapes?
	  ○ An image uploaded from a device?
	  ○ An image found on the web?
	• Add and move text boxes:
	  ○ Manipulate size of text box and font?
	  ○ Copy/paste text from source material or compose original text in the text box?
		• Conduct image searches and select items that advance the argument?
		• Create original images that advance the argument?
		• Represent numerical data in the most compelling way for an argument (e.g., percentages, graphs, charts, or tables)?
		• Compose text that explains the images and data or advances the story?

Table 4.4 The Craft of Infographics (*continued*)

Craft Element	Ability to Create an Infographic (Procedural Knowledge of Form) To produce the features of an infographic as a particular mode of writing, how do you . . .	Ability to Find and Generate Content for an Infographic (Procedural Knowledge of Substance) To produce the content of an individual infographic, how do you . . .
Design (CRAP)	• Use effective headings or titles? • Compose short sentences or succinct paragraphs? • Select preformed templates or create them? **C**ontrast • Use color, space, fonts, and position of elements purposefully to create contrasts that help readers to focus quickly? • Use white/neutral space to balance the overall composition? **R**epetition • Use consistent design elements and/or templates to create cohesion? **A**lignment • Align elements to create a cleaner effect? **P**roximity • Group related or similar items together?	• Compose a headline that reflects the main claim? • Compose subheadings that lead the reader through the story? • Determine how content should be visually placed to best support the argument? • Lay out content so that claims, data, and warrants are clear, if not explicit?
Citation	• Insert links? • Use a particular style guide (e.g., MLA)? • Include citations without taking attention away from the main content of the infographic?	• Manage sources and citation info using organizational tools that allow for later access?

in every category. However, as we have repeated throughout this book, being able to produce a form or to recognize its elements is not the hallmark of digital literacy. Students must be able to deconstruct and craft arguments of substance, so it is important for us to assess Lara's ability to find and/or generate content for her infographic.

Generating content for any form of writing falls in the lower right-hand quadrant of the "inquiry cube"; it is, in fact, the heart of the matter, as it represents inquiry itself. As we consider the procedural knowledge of substance Lara needs to make an argument in her infographic, we realize that creating infographics allows students to engage in inquiry in interesting ways. For instance, Lara cites several sources for her work, including NoKidHungry.org (a campaign that is "ending child hunger in America by ensuring all children get the healthy food they need, every day"), FoodRepublic.com (a site that "explores the culture of food through stories, interviews, global conversations, and experiences,"), the *New York Times*' blog *Well*, and content from the (former) Yahoo! Voices contributor network. Her inclusion of data from these sources shows her ability to search the Internet to find resources that relate to her topic and provide evidence for her claim.

We also see that she uses multiple forms of evidence, including statistics and scientific facts (e.g., "your body will go into starvation mode"). Additionally, she has used the overall design of the piece to guide the reader through the "story" of the infographic, with the main claim about the necessity of breakfast in the main column, and additional information to either side. One might even suggest that visual similarities between the stack of pancakes on the left side of the infographic and the text in the main column are intentional, implying that the main column is a substantial "stack" of information to support the infographic's central argument.

As critical readers of this infographic, however, we wonder about the inquiry that led to this argument. Did Lara conduct primary source research by surveying or interviewing individuals about their eating habits? This kind of data would help set the purpose of this argument. We also wonder about her warranting of the statistical data to her main claim. We might expect those warrants to be made explicitly in the sidebar, but instead, Lara chooses to present new claims without evidence, thus moving the reader away from her main point.

Given these limitations in the argument, we can assess Lara's procedural knowledge of substance and make the following learning goals for her next task:

- Conduct primary source research by surveying or interviewing her classmates.

- Connect all evidence to the claim.

- Stay focused on one claim at a time.

A Word About Sources and Inquiry

We would like to pause here to consider the issue of inquiry and how creating an infographic might allow students to expand the kinds of inquiry they do in the classroom.

We think that it is worth separating research into two types: conducting primary research and accessing existing data. In primary research, students gather their own data, and to do so, they need to consider what types of data will help them develop an argument. Do they need statistical data that helps to answer particular questions, or do they want anecdotal data that provides context? Creating Likert-scale, yes/no, or multiple-choice questions and surveying people will generate numbers that can be represented by statistics. A tool such as Google Forms allows students to easily create and distribute this kind of survey. Once results are gathered, students need to disaggregate the data and consider how to present it in the infographic. Interdisciplinary gateway activities in gathering and presenting data would be important.

When collecting data from other sources, we can have students simply incorporate statistics, quotes from experts, or other forms of evidence that have been published elsewhere. Alternatively, we can have them analyze data that is provided in existing data sets, such as that from the U.S. Census Bureau, the Centers for Disease Control, the U.S. Department of Education, or other nongovernmental sources such as the Pew Research Center. These kinds of tasks could be designed for upper-level students with an expectation that—beyond simply pulling statistics from other sources—they do some mathematical analysis of their own and use their results in the infographic. For the most part, students will be taking existing results and integrating them into their infographics, much like the work that Lara did to demonstrate, using multiple sources, that breakfast is the most important meal of the day.

Practical Matters: How Does a Writer Attend to Issues of Citation, Plagiarism, and Fair Use When Crafting Infographics?

The conventions on citations differ. Publishers and publications use different style guides, most commonly APA, MLA, and Chicago. Most schools have adopted a particular style for citation format. The only constant seems to be that no matter what level we teach, citation format plagues our students.

As students navigate a sea of information, learning to curate sources so that they can locate information later is fundamental to growth as a reader and writer. In the past decade, many tools have been created to help students with the onerous process of citation formatting. A common complaint we hear from librarians (and students) is that no single tool is perfect. We actually think the imperfection is a strength; it requires students to check the formatting, not simply accept it. Using a bibliographic management tool requires attention to detail, and this skill is important to develop.

For this reason we recommend focusing on issues of *citing* (the verb)—and not just *citation* (the noun), which is often coupled with the inherent problem of plagiarism—by teaching students how to use bibliographic management tools that help them to curate a library of citations, not just to list citations in a standard APA or MLA format. While those formatting conventions are important, the main focus for teaching students about citations should be to help them understand how employing outside sources can help make arguments. Or, as Graff and Birkenstein (2009) describe it in their book, *"They Say / I Say": The Moves That Matter in Academic Writing*, we need to help our students learn how to enter the ongoing conversation. No argument exists in a vacuum, and teaching students that they are putting the ideas of others into conversation with their own can help reframe the way we teach why and how to cite sources.

So, with that preface in mind, let's return to the focus of this chapter. Infographics, in particular, offer us an interesting space to think about the nature of citation with digital arguments. For instance, how do we cite the numbers that we generate from a particular data set? What is it that we need to cite when using a data set from the CDC or Pew Research?

We have seen infographics that, like Lara's, refer readers to a list of sources available on a separate page, formatted in MLA or APA style. We have also seen infographics that cite a single source, or point readers to another website for more information. Infographics that present original research typically identify the research project, funder, and date of data collection somewhere on the page. Some just include a list of hyperlinks with nothing more in the way of explanation.

Because there is no standard form for citation in infographics, we recommend having students document their sources in a variety of ways so they will have all the information they need, when they need it, to make a list of references. More importantly, however, we suggest that you teach students how to *curate*—to consciously organize and annotate—their sources. By demonstrating the purpose for citing sources as a way to enter the academic conversation and by teaching students how to use the appropriate tools for the job, we can both promote originality and prevent plagiarism in the process of writing, rather than by playing "gotcha" at the end with a tool that checks for copied text in a student's essay. Put another way, Rebecca Moore Howard suggests that we rethink the ways that we define plagiarism and how to teach students about it:

> *Plagiarism has long been a concern of educators, but that concern has exponentially heightened in the environment of networked text. Some have responded by appealing to students' sense of personal integrity and community ethics; others, by using technology to police students' use of sources. Still others have perceived shifts in textuality itself, occasioned by new literacies; these educators search for revised ways of understanding the production and circulation of text—and thus new ways of mentoring students' relationship with sources. (n.d., Online)*

As Howard suggests, rather than policing students' efforts, we agree that the nature of textuality has changed. In short, students don't go to the library with a stack of 3x5 cards anymore, and we need to change our teaching practices accordingly.

With this focus on the *why* of citing in mind, let's consider a number of tools that students can use to document their research process: productivity tools, social curation tools, and bibliography managers.

Productivity Tools

Designed as applications that can be used across many devices and platforms, most productivity tools have the aim of making our work more efficient. With options that include color-coding information, clipping text and images from the web, adding one's own notes or audio recordings, and being able to share with colleagues, tools such as Microsoft OneNote, Google Keep, and Evernote empower users to be more efficient. By creating different collections, or "notebooks," a writer can gather all of this information into one space and then quickly browse or search for specific details. Thus, one major benefit to using a productivity tool is that a connected reader (Turner and Hicks 2015) can quickly save items to use for her digital writing, keeping a visual context (and images themselves) easily accessible.

One challenge, however—at least from our basic understanding of these products—is that because of the way these tools gather and organize the metadata from sources, exporting information into a standard list of references that follows MLA or APA style is not automatically available. So while they are visually appealing and allow for a great deal of flexibility, these tools are not necessarily the best ones to use if a teacher wants students to move directly from gathering information to citing it.

Social Curation Tools

A number of social media tools can be used to curate materials from a variety of websites into a single, aesthetically pleasing space. One of the original—and still useful—tools from this category is Diigo. As a social bookmarking tool, Diigo allows users to save URLs from various devices and collect them in cloud-based storage. Additionally, users can annotate web pages with virtual sticky notes and highlighting tools. Users can also set up groups so they can see shared annotations available only within the group, using the sticky notes as a space for an ongoing conversation. Finally, a user can see his list of saved URLs and search through them with keywords or tags, though Diigo does not use a visual interface that shows related images.

Additional curation tools have emerged in the past few years with the rise of Pinterest. As a primarily visual interface, Pinterest allows users to create collections of "pins" from various websites, marked with a particular image from that website, as virtual bulletin boards. The boards allow users to get a quick visual overview of the content being presented, and then "repin" it to their own boards. Additionally, users can comment on one another's pins and, if provided the right context and encouragement, use the pins as a space for conversation. Although many teachers and students use Pinterest, it is often blocked by school filters. Two alternative tools are Learnist and Scoop.it!

Like the productivity tools described above, these social curation tools are cloud-based, accessible on many devices, and open for collaboration. Similarly, they lack the ability to easily export metadata into a standard MLA or APA format. So, while they are visually appealing and can be used for initial brainstorming, as students move into the more formal process of writing they will need to use a different set of tools.

Bibliography Managers

The final category of tools useful for tracking and managing online sources is bibliography managers. Sometimes called "reference management software," "bibliography management software," or "citation management software," the general purpose of these tools is clear. Designed to keep track of basic bibliographic facts (title, author, date, and so forth), these database-driven tools allow users to input additional notes or quotes from their sources and then easily export the lists into MLA, APA, Chicago, or other styles. Many of these tools—because they are web-based—also have browser add-ons, and some even have mobile apps. Each is designed to help students identify their sources, capture relevant bibliographic metadata from websites, and then cite that information correctly.

Examples of these types of tools seem to pop up all the time. Many experienced teachers might recall the early days of using EasyBib (which has progressed a great deal), where students would enter the bibliographic information one field at a time and then, with the click of a button, the citation would be produced in MLA style. Now, tools like EasyBib, RefME, Citelighter, ReadCube, and EndNote Basic work well with the data-rich web, extracting appropriate bibliographic information from websites with the click of a button on a web browser.

More advanced tools exist as well, some with a cost and others available for free. For instance, Troy has used the free tool Zotero, produced by the Roy Rosenzweig Center for History and New Media at George Mason University, for nearly a decade. In fact, all the citations in this manuscript—over 100—were imported from metadata on the web (such as a journal article's home page or a book's page on Amazon), and then inserted into the Word document with one click. Then, as we neared the end of manuscript production, Troy clicked another button on the Zotero toolbar and, almost instantly, an entire list of references was generated. There were a few typos (either imported from the original metadata or through our own mistakes when entering additional bibliographic data) as well as spots to clean up capitalization, italicizing, and punctuation. Still, using the bibliographic manager saved hours of time for us as digital writers, and could do the same for our students, too.

Taking It to the Classroom

As always, teaching digital genres and modes is not about tools. We do not want students simply to read and write infographics; rather, we want them to read and write the *arguments* that infographics present to the world. Because infographics require students to do content-rich research and to take a position on an issue, they are well suited for interdisciplinary inquiry. A few ideas for the classroom:

- Compare infographics that take up arguments in different disciplines (e.g., global warming, immigration, best books of all time). Ask students to deconstruct the arguments by determining the kinds of claims being made, the types of evidence used, and the sources cited. Decide whether there are any trends across disciplines or whether there are discipline-specific ways of making arguments.

- Identify a local issue of importance to the school or community. Design a survey and distribute it through social media. Using the data that is collected, have students take a stand and create infographics to share.

- As part of a larger research project, have students design an infographic to represent their inquiry. This infographic can be submitted as its own product to a content-area teacher and as part of a multigenre research project in their English language arts class.

• Invite younger students to search for an infographic using Google Images. Then, to demonstrate how an infographic is typically built in the context of a written argument, ask students to first click on "View Image" and note the URL. Quite literally, where does this infographic live on the Internet? Whose website houses it? Then, ask students to click on "Visit Page." Again, note the URL, and ask, "What additional information can we gain about this infographic from looking at it on this page?"

CHAPTER 5

THE MOVES OF ARGUMENT IN VIDEO

Videos come in many forms: Full-scale Hollywood films. Documentaries with authentic photos and original reel footage. Presentations recorded as screencasts. Six-second Vine videos posted to social media. Each of these types of video employs the medium in different ways, to different audiences, and for different purposes.

Videos can also simply include a series of images that are linked together in a timeline to scroll across a screen. Programs such as Windows Movie Maker or iMovie, or web-based tools such as Animoto or WeVideo, offer this kind of timeline setup that allows a user to quickly drag and drop photos or video clips into a certain order, and then layer in music and narration. As movie-making programs for computers, apps for tablets, and websites for both become ubiquitous, the opportunities to use video as a medium for argument expands exponentially.

It is in this broader context of programs and possibilities that Betsy Reid, who was introduced in Chapter 2, asked her seniors to create a video for an American Rhetoric speech analysis. Rather than just writing the analysis as an alphabetic text, she encouraged them to include short quotations, images, documents, and music to argue how the author used literary devices to appeal to the audience. She had them begin by reviewing the American Rhetoric website (www.americanrhetoric.com/) and then choosing a speech to analyze, identifying unfamiliar vocabulary and noting at least twenty schemes, tropes, and appeals. Students were able to then, quite literally, bring their own voice into the dialogue around great speeches.

Figure 5.1 Screenshot from Daniel's Video

One student, Daniel, selected "Duty, Honor, Country" by General Douglas MacArthur. In his final video, he paired images with quotations from the general's speech to support the claim that MacArthur crafted a "riveting speech that shook every soldier down to his core." For example, in one frame, his narration highlights both the text and the image on the screen: "You can see the soldiers walking through the very wet and dreary terrain when he uses the quote 'dripping dusk to drizzling dawn.'" The image Daniel selected revealed a "wet and dreary terrain" and helped to appeal emotionally to the viewer, thus increasing the effectiveness of his argument. (See Figure 5.1.) Noting the specific requirements that Betsy asked of her students—especially the idea that they use short quotes and illustrative images—the evidence that Daniel chose for his video does support the claim that MacArthur's speech is rhetorically effective.

One additional note of interest: students could potentially download the entire speech and then—using an audio editing tool like Audacity—take small slices of audio to embed in their own video. Imagine, for instance, Daniel's video with a few selected clips from MacArthur's speech layered with the images and words on the screen. While this could seem like a simple embellishment, we would contend that layering in the audio—as another piece of evidence—could provide a unique way for Daniel, or any of Betsy's students, to support their own argument about the rhetorical effectiveness of the speech.

Looking at it another way, we can compare the kind of digital writing from Betsy's class to the work done by students in Lauren King's classroom; instead of creating a rhetorical analysis, her tenth graders crafted arguments that included still images, moving video, and alphabetic text utilizing the mode of public service announcements (PSAs). Like many smartphone users today, they created their videos entirely on their mobile devices since they have limited access to computers and laptops. The students used live action shots of themselves for the main parts of the PSAs, and then supplemented those video clips with additional text and statistics. Like Daniel's analysis of a text, by crafting an argument and supporting it with features of digital video, these PSAs are arguments too, though they take a different approach to making claims and using evidence. We will explore the mode of PSAs—and the work of Lauren's students—later in the chapter.

The range of argumentative modes for video has become increasingly rich. We know that many teachers have employed genres such as commercials and documentaries or journalistic forms such as interviews, newscasts, or talk shows. Returning to Lunsford et al.'s (2013) belief that "everything's an argument," we could say that all kinds of video—whether a science fiction thriller on the big screen or a recording of a young woman graduating from high school that her family has posted on YouTube—are presenting claims, evidence, and warrants. While this book focuses on texts that were, indeed, designed as arguments, it is worth noting that many of the critiques we offer for argumentative videos can be applied to all kinds of film and videos because—even if they are a narrative genre—they are presenting an implicit argument.

As we've noted in previous chapters, our aim is to help students focus on the argument they are making. It is not that they are making a video; they are using the medium of video to make an argument, just as they could make an argument with alphabetic text on screen or paper. However, video provides a number of affordances that can support argument, so our goal is for students to deconstruct videos, understand common craft elements of video, and then be able to remix existing video elements—as well as create their own.

Characteristics and Content: What Do Videos Look Like?

We have all seen countless videos, from short clips to full TV shows or films. By some estimates (Nielsen 2014), the average American will watch television (or video) up to five hours a day (though, in our multitasking age, we wonder how much *critical* viewing happens). Still, the point is clear: nearly everyone is familiar with the tropes of video. And in these various modes, we have seen a variety of techniques for making a claim, some of them implicit and others explicit. Consider a few examples:

- Ken Burns, the noted documentary filmmaker, has noted that "all story is manipulation. Is there acceptable manipulation? You bet." (2012). He uses a variety of techniques, including panning and zooming on still images as well as the narrator's voice, additional interviews, and dramatic music to create a certain effect.

- Media literacy scholars have, for decades, encouraged teachers and students to critically read/view implicit and explicit messages. For instance, Renee Hobbs and her colleagues at the Media Education Lab have recently launched a website, Mind Over Media, that offers a succinct list of how to recognize propaganda techniques: "Activating strong emotions," "Responding to audience needs & values," "Simplifying information & ideas," and "Attacking opponents."

- Finally, after decades of criticism, a number of fashion companies such as American Eagle and magazines such as *Seventeen* have explicitly stated that they will change their stance on photo manipulation of models, though some critics don't believe these policy changes make much difference.

In just this brief glimpse, the power of visual media is clear: moving or still pictures, narration and music, and the gaze of the camera all combine to make an immediate, and important, effect on viewers. Moreover, as Troy documented in *Crafting Digital Writing* (2013), there are a number of craft elements that go into the creation of a digital video, and probably many more that could be added. (See Table 5.1.)

Table 5.1 Craft Elements in Digital Video

Cinematic Techniques	Documentary Techniques
• Camera angle • Cuts/transitions • Focus (near, mid, far) • Framing • Gaze • Establishing shot • Pan • Zoom	• Voice-over • Interviews • Archival footage • Reconstructions • Montage • Exposition

Thus, as digital writers who compose video-based arguments, we must teach our students how to, in Ken Burns' words, rely on "acceptable manipulation" and not move into the realm of propaganda and deception.

As we consider the declarative knowledge needed to construct a video, we will focus on PSAs (see Table 5.2). Many of these characteristics would apply to other modes, but you would want to consider each in isolation. For example, literary analysis videos created by Betsy's students would not have the PSA feature of being brief, usually sixty seconds or less.

Commercials and PSAs rely on emotional appeals (noted in the declarative knowledge of substance column)—in particular, ethos and pathos, two of the Aristotelian appeals of argument. Still, we want to make sure that students—in reading and in writing—move past the appeals alone and dig deeper into conversations about the evidence, warrants, and claims being made. To do this, we must return our focus to Toulmin's vision of argument.

What Constitutes a Claim, Evidence, Warrant, and Attention to Rebuttal in a Video?

As a means of exploring argument in video, let's view an ad that made a specific claim, and inspired a great deal of controversy along the way: Coca-Cola's 2014 Super

Table 5.2 Characteristics and Content of PSAs

Conventional Characteristics of a PSA (Declarative Knowledge of Form)	Content of a PSA (Declarative Knowledge of Substance)
• Typically brief, just 15 to 60 seconds • Typically includes a memorable tagline • May use animation, live action, or other combinations of video options • May use images, music, sound effects, or narration in an evocative manner • May include a metaphorical representation (such as the frying egg in the "This is your brain on drugs" campaign)	• Clearly (though often metaphorically) introduces a problem and offers a solution • Provides evidence of the problem and its effects on an individual, family, or community • Provides information on additional resources such as a phone number or website • Often speaks in the second person, encouraging the viewer to take action • May include emotional appeals

Bowl commercial. Titled "It's Beautiful," the ad includes a series of brief video clips that range from a cowboy on his horse to teenagers tap dancing on a sidewalk to a young woman wearing a headscarf. As these short video clips play, the song "America the Beautiful" is sung in the background, beginning with words in English and then, as the verse continues, shifting into different languages. Coca-Cola described the ad in this manner: "'It's Beautiful' was created to celebrate Coke moments among all Americans who together enjoy ice-cold, refreshing Coke. The ad provides a snapshot of the real lives of Americans representing diverse ethnicities, religions, races and families, all found in the United States."

Using this statement from Coca-Cola, we have analyzed the video by highlighting specific pieces of evidence that were employed, as well as the underlying warrants that connect them to a claim. (See Table 5.3.)

Table 5.3 Example of Evidence and Warrant in a Commercial

Claim: Every American—regardless of race, class, gender, or cultural background—enjoys Coke.	
Evidence	**Warrant**
Images of Americans from various geographic regions, cultural backgrounds, races, genders, and occupations all participating in a variety of activities	If Americans of all backgrounds and experiences drink Coke, then everyone likely enjoys it.
The song "America the Beautiful" being sung in many different languages	If Coke is associated with "America the Beautiful" and a variety of languages, Americans of all backgrounds most likely value it.
Explicit placement of the Coke brand—cup in movie theater, bottles on the table, a cooler in the background, glasses at a restaurant, a street vendor, bottle caps in the pool, the painted wall—throughout the ad	Because Coke is everywhere, we can reason that most Americans likely enjoy it.

The "It's Beautiful" ad immediately set the Internet ablaze with both compliments and criticism, particularly from individuals who do not value a multilingual, multicultural nation. In other words, the warrants that the Coke advertisers intended were not shared by all who viewed it. These critics warranted the evidence—particularly the multilingual interpretation of "America the Beautiful"—to form a different argument. This example reminds us of the difficulty in crafting digital arguments in video and in considering counters to those arguments. While Coca-Cola may have been attempting to use emotional appeals (e.g., the use of "America the Beautiful" to tap into emotions of harmony), the evidence they chose to include had different effects on different audiences. These effects may have been inspired by the individual's acceptance (or not) of the underlying warrants.

The ability to critique advertisements—by articulating the claims they are presenting, the evidence used to support the claims, and the warrants that must be accepted for the argument to work—is a key component of developing both digital and media literacies. However, we also want students to deconstruct and compose other types of video-based arguments. We have already named many possibilities, and each type will have genre-based characteristics. For the sake of simplicity, we will focus the rest of this chapter on public service announcements, as this genre forms the basis of many video-based arguments created in school. We hope that our analysis of PSAs provide a model for deconstructing other video-based genres as well.

The Craft of Composing: What Does a Student Need to Know and Be Able to Do to Read and Write a PSA?

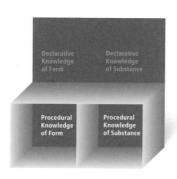

In their minute-long PSA, "Don't Ruin Your Image" (Figure 5.2), students in Lauren's class began their video with a young woman typing a message into her phone at school and, we can presume, hitting "send." She then stands up and heads to the girls' restroom, where she enters a stall and tosses her blouse over the wall. A few moments pass while, we presume, she snaps a picture and sends it. Subtle piano music plays in the background and no words are spoken in this first part of the video.

Figure 5.2 Screenshots from Student Video

Then, forty seconds in, the video switches to a scene of two young men talking in the hallway with their friends, overlaid with the words, "Don't let someone else fool you." One young man is looking at the phone and showing it to his friend, who says, excitedly, "Send me that! Send me that!" At forty-five seconds, the scene cuts to the original actress walking up to a pair of friends. They admonish

her for sharing pictures such as these and tell her to "go away." Finally, the words "Stop Sexting" and "Don't ruin your image" roll across the screen.

The students were able to illustrate their point in a succinct manner. As evidence, they demonstrated how this young woman's friends, both male and female, would react. By showing how quickly an image, especially an inappropriate one, can spread through social media and mobile devices, these digital writers were able to convey how an attempt to be flirtatious could "ruin your image." (As a reminder, the link to this video, and all digital student work, can be found on the companion wiki.)

These digital writers could have made a number of additional moves, using various craft elements to enhance their message. For instance, how might their PSA have been different if they had:

- Included statistical information about the number of teens who use social media regularly and have mobile devices?

- Recorded the dialogue with a better microphone, making the admonitions from the friends more clear at the end?

- Maintained a horizontal orientation for the camera?

- Included some type of misconception about the ways in which images on social media can "disappear" after a certain amount of time?

- Made the transitions either more subtle or more drastic, to accentuate the emotional intensity?

- Used a closing shot to show the young woman's reaction to her mistake?

As we look closely at the video produced by Lauren's students, we can see areas where they have mastered skills and others where they might develop their procedural knowledge to better craft the argument. For example, the students were able to create the original video using their mobile devices, trimming and editing video to create visual media that serve as logical evidence. They added text in the form of an overlay to highlight their claim. However, they could improve their use of available technology to capture higher-quality audio that would further enhance their evidence. They might also consider expanding the kinds of evidence they include, either with voice-overs or text, to bolster their argument. At the same time, though, we might consider the students' strong audience awareness; perhaps their focus on emotional appeals was a carefully considered approach uniquely honed for their audience. In other words, was the omission of logical appeals such as statistics and research data intentional because the students did not feel that those elements would matter to their audience?

The craft elements presented in Table 5.4 articulate many of the skills that students need to create effective PSAs.

Table 5.4 The Craft of Digital Video

Craft Element	The Ability to Create a Video (Procedural Knowledge of Form) To produce the features of a video as a particular mode of argument writing, how do you. . .	The Ability to Find and Generate Content for a Video (Procedural Knowledge of Substance) To produce the content of an individual video designed to make an argument, how do you. . .
Video clips and still images	• Film original video or take original pictures? • Find existing videos and pictures in an appropriate format for importing? • Trim video clips for length? • Crop photos? • Apply effects such as slow motion, filters, speeding up?	• Select or create visual media to serve as logical evidence? • Select or create media to underscore the claim? • Select or create media that appeal to ethos, logos, or pathos?
Text in written form: titles, captions, quotes, statistics, etc.	• Add text in the form of overlays, captions, title screens, or animations? • Balance the amount of text with the amount of space available on the screen (full screen with solid background, one-third of screen as caption, etc.)?	• Determine when to include alphabetic text? • Show a graph, chart, infographic, or table? • Show a quote from an expert?
Text in oral form: voice-over	• Write a script and record as an audio file? • Insert and layer audio into the video?	• Adjust tone, pacing, and style to best represent the argument? • Pause and inflect effectively? • Select and/or create a "persona"? • Take a stance as a speaker? • Determine the perspective of the narrator?

Table 5.4 The Craft of Digital Video (*continued*)

Craft Element	The Ability to Create a Video (Procedural Knowledge of Form) To produce the features of a video as a particular mode of argument writing, how do you. . .	The Ability to Find and Generate Content for a Video (Procedural Knowledge of Substance) To produce the content of an individual video designed to make an argument, how do you. . .
Transitions and filters	• Add appropriate transitions such as a "fade to black" or "page turn"? • Add appropriate filters such as "sepia" or "vintage film"?	• Use transitions to further the argument or accentuate a point by making it slow, normal, or fast? • Use filters to demonstrate shifts in time or perspective?
Audio: music and sound effects	• Create or choose music and/or sound effects to accentuate the narration?	• Select appropriate musical genres, create clips of that music with an audio editor? • Adjust volume or tone of music? • Include appropriate sound effects to aurally illustrate an action or process?

Practical Matters: How Does a Writer Attend to Issues of Citation, Plagiarism, and Fair Use When Crafting Video?

As digital writing becomes more and more a part of the English language arts curriculum, we need to give particular attention to issues of citation and plagiarism as well as copyright and fair use. Our colleague and mentor Renee Hobbs reminds us that, while closely related, proper citation and plagiarism are *ethical* concerns and copyright and fair use are *legal* issues. In her book *Copyright Clarity*, she provides a brief example:

Although the conduct of plagiarism may overlap with copyright infringement, the two concepts are distinct. You can plagiarize from Shakespeare, but you'll never have a copyright problem since his works are in the public domain. Plagiarism is an ethical problem handled by teachers in schools; copyright infringement is a legal problem handled by the courts. (2010, p. 8)

As we described in Chapter 3, as long as the use of the work is transformative, you and your students have wide latitude when incorporating copyrighted materials into your digital writing. That said, there are alternative forms of copyright that do not adhere to quite the same rules as fair use, most notably those that are licensed via Creative Commons and those available in the public domain. You may hear someone speak about materials that are licensed in these alternative formats (that is, not the "Big C," all-rights-reserved kind of copyright) as "copyleft" materials. Copyleft, according to *Wikipedia*, one of the largest sources of materials available with a public license, is

a form of licensing, and can be used to maintain copyright conditions for works ranging from computer software, to documents, to art . . . under copyleft, an author may give every person who receives a copy of the work permission to reproduce, adapt, or distribute it, with the accompanying requirement that any resulting copies or adaptations are also bound by the same licensing agreement.

Let's look at both Creative Commons and public domain materials in more detail.

Creative Commons

Founded in 2001, Creative Commons (CC) offers authors, photographers, musicians, filmmakers, and other creative individuals the ability to share and license works with a specialized form of copyright, allowing for degrees of protection for the original creator while opening up the material for others to use as well. Lawrence Lessig, a professor of law at Harvard and author of several books about intellectual property in the digital age, describes CC in this way:

Creative Commons gives authors free tools—legal tools (copyright licenses) and technical tools (metadata and simple marking technology)—to mark their creativity with the freedoms they intend it to carry. So if you're a teacher, and you want people to share your work, CC gives you a tool to signal this to others. Or if you're a photographer and don't mind if others collect your work, but don't want Time *magazine to take your work without your permission, then CC would give you a license to signal this. All the licenses express the relevant freedoms in three separate layers: one, a "commons deed" that expresses the freedoms associated with the content in a human readable form; two, the "legal code," that is the actual copyright licenses; and three, metadata surrounding the content that expresses the freedoms contained within that copyright license in terms computers can understand. These three layers work together to make the freedoms associated with the creative work clear. Not all freedoms, but some. Not "All Rights Reserved" but "Some Rights Reserved."* (2009, pp. 277–278)

Thus, a CC license offers creators a range of choices, from having his or her work copyrighted (with very limited options for reuse such as only for noncommercial purposes) all the way to completely open, requiring only attribution to the original source when reused. There are individuals and organizations who do, without compensation or attribution, put their work in the public domain, as we will shortly describe in more detail. For the moment, it is worth noting that there are conditions on a CC-licensed work that a creator can alter to his or her preference:

- Attribution: All CC licenses include, at a minimum, the "attribution" requirement, noting that you should give credit to the original creator of the work.

- Noncommercial: Some CC-licensed materials include this requirement, noting that the original work can be remixed or used, but cannot be used for commercial gain.

- Share-Alike: Some creators want to make sure that their work is used in the spirit of sharing and therefore put a "share-alike" license on their work so anyone using it will, in turn, be required to continuing sharing.

- No-Derivatives: Some creators will choose this option to ensure that the original creative work is shared in its entirety.

No matter what the CC license specifications include, it is worth it to draw the distinction between when and how we use various materials and how we cite them. As with any materials, including references for one's own project is important, and CC-licensed work—while free to use—should still be cited appropriately. For instance, Troy found the image shown in Figure 5.3 on Flickr to use in a blog post. While he could create a full academic citation in APA format, he instead makes a digital writing move to reference the source.

Notice in this screenshot how Troy has cited the image. In the caption, he wrote: "Some rights reserved by Barrett.Discovery." But the real reference comes in the craft of digital writing; by including a hyperlink to the original picture's page on Flickr, Troy points readers of his blog back to the image's source, where the photographer Laurie Sullivan, under the name Barrett.Discovery, has invited others to use her photo with an "Attribution" license. This license allows Troy to use the image on his blog (and, for that matter, in this book) as long as attribution is given and with no other restrictions on it, such as being limited for noncommercial use

(Advance) Response to Pre-Service Teachers' Questions about Technology

Posted on **February 21, 2015**

— Some rights reserved by Barrett.Discovery

This coming Monday night, I have been invited to join Sean Connors' preservice teachers at the University of Arkansas through a conversation on Google Hangouts. They created a very smart list of questions for me, and in order to maximize our time, I've written this brief response with lots of links, some of which we can explore together or, more likely, students can review on their own after our chat.

Here is my response to their questions:

Figure 5.3 Screenshot from Troy's Blog

only. Also, since the picture itself is a link back to the original page on Flickr, there is no long and obtrusive URL, or even a shortened URL from a tool like Bit.ly. Troy has instead made the image itself the point of reference.

However, if that picture ever appears in a book, as it does in this one, he would also want to include a citation such as this:

> Sullivan, L. 2013. DSC06585, November 25. *www.flickr.com/photos/ projectdiscovery/12373788014/sizes/s/.*

Lessig's point about copyright and attribution is simple: old models of copyright no longer hold true in a digital world. Though it is another form of copyright, Creative Commons allows creators and users of materials a number of freedoms that traditional copyright and fair use cannot match. The best place to find CC-licensed works is the CC website itself: creativecommons.org/search.

Public Domain

Items available in the public domain are different from those protected by copyright and Creative Commons. In short, you can use public domain materials in any way that you see fit. Remember, while it is legally appropriate to use these materials in all manners, it is still ethically and academically appropriate to cite them. Again, as he would with the CC image above, if Troy were to find a public domain picture for his blog, he would embed the image with a link back to the original source, such as Wikimedia Commons or the Library of Congress.

Many resources are available in the public domain from the U.S. government, including images from the Library of Congress (www.flickr.com/photos/library_of_congress /sets/), the National Parks (www.nature.nps.gov/multimedia.cfm), and NASA (www .nasa.gov/multimedia/imagegallery/index.html). Other popular resources include the Internet Archive (https://archive.org/), Wikimedia Commons (https://commons .wikimedia.org/wiki/Main_Page), and the CIA World Factbook (https://www.cia.gov /library/publications/resources/the-world-factbook/index.html). Finally, in terms of finding copyleft materials, one incredible resource is Joyce Valenza's wiki site, Copyright Friendly. Here, she has collected over a hundred links to various sources for CC- and public domain-licensed materials that you and your students can use: https://copy rightfriendly.wikispaces.com/.

Taking It to the Classroom

Introducing students and, quite often, teachers to the concept of composing video can sometimes be a daunting task. While more and more of us are becoming familiar with tools such as iMovie, WeVideo, and other video editing programs, Troy has found that giving people—children, adolescents, and adults—an opportunity to play with a video editing task in a low-stakes manner is often a good way to introduce bigger projects such as digital stories or public service announcements. In this lesson, adapted from Penny Lew, one of his colleagues at the Chippewa River Writing Project, Troy invites people to create thirty-second nursery rhymes as a gateway activity for producing longer videos.

First, Troy shows a very brief digital story or PSA created by a teacher or student, depending on the audience. For a good variety of selections, one source with many examples of digital stories is the University of Houston's Educational Uses of Digital Storytelling site.

As participants watch, he asks them to identify the various types of media elements that constitute video: still images, video segments, text in the form of titles and captions, voice-over narration, and background music. As he makes a brief list on a whiteboard or in a word-processing document, Troy quickly reviews each of these elements and explains how—as a form of evidence contributing to an argument or advancing a storyline—they combine to make a successful digital video.

At this point, one logical move would be to invite participants to begin thinking about their own digital story or PSA. However, Troy moves in a different direction. Rather than having participants jump right into the process of brainstorming, storyboarding, and producing their own digital video, Troy presents a simple challenge: for the next twenty or thirty minutes (depending on the time available), everyone will create a digital video version of a nursery rhyme. Limiting the subject matter to something short that the participants already know well helps them to focus on aspects of video composition, not content. To help the group fully understand this process, Troy models it first.

Imagine, for instance, that Troy selects "Humpty Dumpty" as his nursery rhyme. He begins by doing a quick image search to find images that represent Humpty Dumpty. As he searches for the images and downloads them to the computer, he also leads a very brief think-aloud about copyright and fair use for educational purposes.

He then talks about the ways in which students and teachers could create their own media to supplement existing materials, which he promises to demonstrate.

Once the images are downloaded, he then shows how to import them into the movie-making program. Along with showing different ways in which the videos can be imported into the timeline, Troy demonstrates a few of the transitions—such as fade to black, screen dissolve, or a turning page—and talks about the rhetorical effect of each one. Knowing that this nursery rhyme will be only a few seconds long, he also discusses whether or not too many transitions could be distracting. Troy then moves on to adding sound.

First, Troy demonstrates how to record narration. Depending on how much time he has, he may show participants how to record narration with a smartphone, or just record directly into the computer. Wanting to emphasize the point that the narration can be recorded outside of school, he shows some of the ways in which all of the files can be saved in cloud storage such as Google Drive or Dropbox. Again, depending on the time, Troy will sometimes intentionally mess up the first version of his narration and then rerecord to demonstrate how easy it can be. Also, he may show some of the default musical tracks that could be added to the video, adjusting the audio levels on the narration and the music until they are suitable for listening without being overpowering or drowning one another out.

Once the narration is recorded and added in, Troy returns to the idea of creating his own media. As a way to show that participants can add their own images or video clips to their existing timeline, Troy often records a quick introduction to the nursery rhyme, such as: "I'm Troy Hicks and I will be reading the classic nursery rhyme 'Humpty Dumpty' for you today." Then Troy answers questions from the group and sets a timer to give participants fifteen to twenty minutes to complete their nursery rhyme video.

Troy has used this gateway activity in multiple settings, from individual classrooms to writing project summer institutes to professional development workshops with dozens of teachers in the audience. Each time, invariably, people begin with a healthy amount of skepticism, then jump into the activity, often working together with a partner, and then push forward right up until the timer signals the alarm. While the final products are not perfect—nor are they meant to be—Troy uses this type of activity as a way to introduce the concept of digitally writing video compositions. At the end of the session, after having three or four participants share their nursery rhymes, Troy often takes a few moments to ask people about the process:

- As a digital writer, how did you feel over the last fifteen minutes? Were you anxious? Excited? Engaged?

- What were the specific tasks that you had to engage in so you could complete your video? Let's think about verbs here: what, specifically, did you do? Search? Download? Import? Sequence? Record?

- Also, he will connect the feelings and the actions to a broader conversation about twenty-first-century literacies. He might ask: How did you feel about collaborating? What did you learn about copyright? How else might you share your work with a global audience?

- Given that this was a low-pressure, fun activity, what are the takeaways that you can use in your own classroom? How might you scaffold students in the process of creating digital stories or public service announcements? What additional skills will they need to build? What additional minilessons will you need to plan?

Once the students or teachers have shared their ideas and reflected on the process, Troy transitions out of the activity, reminding them that the digital writing process is a recursive, ongoing process. Although this particular lesson may feel quite linear—especially given that the sequence was to find pictures, then record their voice, and finally add a brief introduction—when engaging in longer, more robust projects, the process of digitally writing a video is never quite so neat.

Still, this nursery rhyme activity allows digital writers of all ages and experience levels the opportunity to simply play, to become immersed in the process. Then, as they begin to think about building a longer, more complex argument, Troy can layer in additional conversations about evidence, warrants, and claims. Much like Humpty Dumpty, all the pieces of a digital argument may not fit nicely together in A-B-C fashion, but at least the initial concerns of how to create a digital video have been addressed.

In addition to the examples shared in this chapter, alternatives for having students create argumentative videos could include these activities:

- Invite students to analyze existing arguments using a video annotation tool such as Vialogues, VoiceThread, or Ponder to describe what they have created and/or to ask questions of their viewers.

- Similarly, once students create their own videos, have them create a "director's cut" using screencasting tools such as Jing, Screencast-O-Matic, or Screencastify, documenting the choices that they have made.

- Alternatively, if the video is designed to be an interactive, quiz-like experience, students could use a tool such as PlayPosit or EDpuzzle to ask their viewers a variety of questions in true/false, multiple-choice, or short-answer format.

CHAPTER 6

THE MOVES OF ARGUMENT IN SOCIAL MEDIA

Janelle Bence's students load the website of KQED, a public broadcasting station out of San Francisco. As an English and humanities teacher at New Tech High @ Coppell in Texas, Janelle (@Janelle) asks her students to navigate to the "Do Now" prompt, this week's topic focusing on "Youth in Participatory Politics." According to KQED, Do Now

> *is a weekly activity for students to engage and respond to current issues using*
> *social media tools like Twitter, Instagram, Tumblr, and Vine. KQED aims to*
> *introduce 21st Century skills and add value to learning through the integration*
> *of relevant local content and new media tools and technologies. Do Now gives*
> *students a chance to practice civic engagement and digital citizenship skills while*
> *they explore ways to connect topics in their classes to the present day. (2016)*

By participating in Do Now, Janelle's students are able to join in conversations with countless others from around the country, adding their voices about contemporary topics such as immigration, elections, and driverless cars. They are able to test claims and defend and refine their arguments in a conversational setting. Later in the chapter, we will introduce you to a series of arguments presented (and defended and refined) by students in a conversation tagged with #DoNowTesting.

For Janelle's students who participated in #DoNowPolitics, the conversation begins on Hackpad, a collaborative writing space. The particular prompt for that week's discussion was posted on KQED's blog: "Do teens today identify with political parties, or are they redefining political action? What does being politically active mean to you? "#DoNowPolitics" (Youth Radio/KQED Education 2016).

Janelle then asked them to consider the following questions and to respond using a meme-like image that incorporated famous quotes:

- What does "politically active" mean?

- Have millennials redesigned what political action looks like? (KQED Do Now, #DoNowPolitics)

- What are effective methods of inspiring such [political] activity to foster civic engagement in teenagers?

- If teens are critical to the future of democracy, how do we encourage their involvement in participatory politics?

One student, Jake, responded by pairing a silhouetted woman with a megaphone and the popular quote: "Inspire the CHANGE you want to see in the world" (Figure 6.1). From what we can tell, the first instance of this image was on Reflection Press'

Figure 6.1 Jake's Original Reply to Janelle's Prompt

website in 2013, with a post entitled "Inspiring Change, Changing History." We assume that Jake remixed this original image into his own.

Jake's initial post received comments from classmates. Jared offered a supportive response: "Love the quote sounds so inspiring and the poster is really eye catching." Then a dialogue emerged between two students, Raed and Anika (see Figure 6.2).

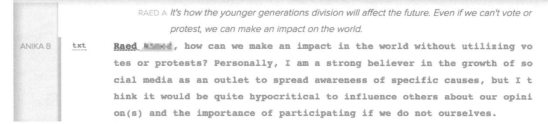

Figure 6.2 Raed and Anika Discuss Jake's Post

This civil exchange included a claim that was challenged, all inspired by the image one student created. This healthy disagreement was both the start of deep conversation and a teachable moment. By engaging students in analyzing their language and the moves they made in their commenting, Janelle could help students to see themselves as critical readers and writers of social media, a stance we feel is vital in today's society.

The Problems of Misinformation and Confirmation Bias

How many times have you seen a "too good to be true" hoax on your social media feed? How many times did you repost the feed, perhaps saying, "Just in case this is true, I'm posting!"

As we were drafting this chapter, our Facebook feeds were overtaken by the following message:

> *According to* Good Morning America, *Not a hoax! Mark Zuckerberg has announced that he is giving away $45 billion of Facebook stock. What you may not have heard is that he plans to give 10% of it away to people like YOU and ME! All you have to do is copy and paste this message into a post*

IMMEDIATELY. At midnight PST, Facebook will search through the day's post
and award 1000 people with $4.5 million Each as a way of saying thank you
for making Facebook such a powerful vehicle for connection. (Chowdhry 2015)

Spoiler alert: it was a hoax.

Nevertheless, it went viral quickly, prompting an article on Forbes.com to assert "Facebook Hoax: Mark Zuckerberg Is Not Giving Away $4.5 Million to 1,000 Users" and to encourage readers to check Snopes to evaluate these kinds of posts before resharing with their networks. On its page "Something for Nothing," Snopes lists dozens of these kinds of hoaxes. Day after day, individuals fall prey to them, hope they are true, and share the misinformation with their friends.

Aside from the embarrassment you might feel if you reposted a "something for nothing" hoax and a friend pointed out your gullibility, little harm may come to you, your family and friends, or your school and community. However, in the introduction of her 2002 book, *Web of Deception: Misinformation on the Internet*, Annie Mintz presented the challenge in stark terms:

In this age of Internet nomads and mass acceptance of online information
on the World Wide Web, what if new dangers emerge not from a lack of
competence by database publishers or searchers but from a malevolent
competence? Dangers like deliberate deception, deliberate misinformation, and
half-truths that can be used to divert a seeker from the real information being
sought. How many ways can people find to use technologies to support lies,
deception, misdirection, fraud, spin control, propaganda, and all other forms
of misdirection? (2002, p. xviii)

Individuals often respond emotionally to what they read in social networks, posting or reposting without critically analyzing the argument being made. Often, we don't recognize that the simple act of sharing information itself makes a claim, positioning us in certain ways—and that those who read what we share can engage in the argument. While sharing misinformation is becoming a societal problem, there are ways to help students become mindful, critical users of social media as well as active producers of accurate information. It may not save the world, but it is a step toward a solution. At the heart of this work, we believe, is the ability to deconstruct and compose arguments in these socially-networked spaces.

Misinformation has become a problem as open access to the Internet allows users to share content that has not been vetted. In fact, the World Economic Forum detailed the global risks of "digital wildfires" in a 2013 report and in another 2014 report ranked the "spread of misinformation" in the top ten challenges facing society. The problem, it seems, is not getting better. To tackle it, however, we must explore what *The Guardian* calls "an emergent field of study" (Vis 2014) and understand how the spread of misinformation works.

A recent study published by the National Academy of Sciences sheds some light on this issue. By analyzing sharing patterns in publicly available Facebook groups, Vicario et al. (2016) found that "users mostly tend to select and share content according to a specific narrative and to ignore the rest" (p. 4). People share within like-minded communities, creating "echo-chambers" that feed "confirmation bias" (p. 4). In short, users tend to share information that comes from sources they trust (e.g., online "friends" or "followers") without challenging the claims, evidence, or warrants that make up the argument. In this way, false information is easily passed from one person to another, accepted broadly by a community, and becomes "highly resistant to correction" (p. 5). Vicario et al. put it in more dire terms: "Users tend to aggregate in communities of interest, which causes reinforcement and fosters confirmation bias, segregation, and polarization. This comes at the expense of the quality of the information and leads to proliferation of biased narratives fomented by unsubstantiated rumors, mistrust, and paranoia" (p. 5).

Both Google and Facebook have changed algorithms to better filter out false news stories and hoaxes. Even so, it is incumbent on users to fact check and think carefully before sharing.

Filter Bubbles

The information we access online is limited by human confirmation bias. As Eli Pariser (2012) argues in *The Filter Bubble: How the New Personalized Web Is Changing What We Read and How We Think*, these same algorithms that are designed to help sift out extraneous information can also limit our worldview. The tools that we trust—like Google, Facebook, and other sites—generate a "filter bubble" around us. In a 2011 TED talk (Pariser 2011), Pariser explained that different users get different— sometimes wildly different—results from the same search. As an example, he contrasted the results two different users received for the word *Egypt* at the height of the 2011 uprisings in the Arab world. One user's top results reflected the then current unrest. Another user's top results offered tourism information. Pariser describes the bubble as invisible, and argues that we do not have an option to opt in or out. We don't even know what we don't know.

Confirmation bias—where people read arguments and look only for data that supports their preconceived notions—is an issue that we can tackle from the classroom. As Vis (2014) argues:

> In this emergent field of study we need solutions that not only help us to better understand how false information spreads online, but also how to deal with it. This requires different types of expertise: a strong understanding of social media combined with an ability to deal with large volumes of data that foreground the importance of human interpretation of information in context.

The solution, we know, is that we must teach our students to become vetters of information. Just as *Wikipedia* controls the spread of misinformation through its users, who document false claims and erroneous facts, we can control the spread of misinformation within our communities by engaging in social media as readers and writers of argument.

A Possible Solution: Engaging as Readers and Writers in Arguments Presented Through Social Media

We have had the privilege of talking to teens around the country about their digital reading practices (Turner and Hicks 2015), and we were not surprised to find that the majority of the reading they do daily consists of "short form" texts—status updates, tweets, text messages (Thompson 2010)—via social networks. However, when we probed further, we realized that they did not view this kind of reading as *reading*. As Catrina said to us in an interview, "If my teacher asks me, like, how much did you read today? It wouldn't be like, 'well, I did twenty minutes on [social media]. I would [just] consider it, like, sitting down [with the device]. If I read a book for twenty minutes, I'd tell her about it." Like many of her peers, Catrina simply did not view reading a text message or Facebook post as reading.

Catrina's comments echo the findings of the Pew Internet and American Life Project study, which reported that teenagers did not view the writing they did in online spaces as "*real* writing" (Lenhart et al. 2008, p. i). But what if we could help students make the pivot to recognize that it is, indeed, reading (or writing)? What if they did approach social media in the same manner as they would any type of text deserving of attention? What if they became critical readers of the arguments that fly by their screens each moment? And what if, in turn, they considered their responses to these posts, thinking about their endorsement of them or the qualifications they might add to the claims presented as they reshared? This type of "connected reading" is, as we have described elsewhere, "the heart of research" (Turner and Hicks 2015).

Take, for instance, a meme that went viral during the epic Powerball craze of January 2016. The meme quite clearly claimed that the $1.3 billion payout of the Powerball lottery could solve poverty. The author provided the following math equation as evidence:

Powerball $1.3 billion

÷ U.S. population 300 million

Everyone receives $4.33 million

Going viral on Instagram and Facebook, the meme was shared by many individuals in our own networks, apparently agreeing with the underlying claim. As the *Huffington Post*, ABC News, CNET, and many other outlets reported quite quickly, this argument included false data. First, the U.S. population at the time was more than 322 million. Second, the math was egregiously wrong (Mazza 2016; Schneider 2016): this equation would in fact leave each American with roughly enough money for a coffee at Starbucks.

Why did so many individuals share this meme without checking the facts? Because they reacted quickly and did not read or write mindfully. This "writing-by-the-way" (Hicks and Perrin 2014) can sometimes be incredibly useful as people are able to share immediate updates about developing situations, natural disasters, or other significant events. Writing-by-the-way can be used for brainstorming and collaborating, developing a shared draft of a text over time, or simply engaging in substantive conversation on a moment-to-moment basis. These quick bursts of writing, we would add, are often arguments—advocating for an idea, drawing in more evidence, making connections to existing arguments and building on them.

However, retweeting, liking, and sharing existing content—especially erroneous content—differ from "writing-by-the-way" and, for that matter, from writing itself. Yet these seemingly simple acts of resharing content can still push forward an argument (even an erroneous one, filled with misinformation), in ways that can be helpful or harmful, depending on one's perspective, contrary to those who claim that "retweets are not endorsements." As reporter Anne Johnson wrote for National Public Radio, "[D]on't retweet anything you wouldn't report yourself" (2014).

What do we want students (and adults, for that matter) to do when they view and compose their own social network posts, be they reviews on product or service sites, comments on blog posts, or status updates? We want them to monitor their reading and writing, analyze the argument being made, and think carefully before sharing with other readers. We want them to consider what it means to reshare a post and, more specifically, what kind of argument they are creating or promoting by doing so.

But social media is fast paced. Tweets, updates, and posts constantly move across the screen, making a user's interaction nearly synchronous. As Clive Thompson (2010) explains: "Today's multitasking tools really do make it harder than before to stay focused during long acts of reading and contemplation. They require a high level of 'mindfulness'— paying attention to your own attention."

In our age of distraction, simply hitting "like" on someone else's post is an endorsement, an act of arguing in the real world. Reading and writing are never neutral activities, and we must encourage students to be mindful as they participate in social media. To build on the mantra: read like a writer, write for a reader, and be mindful of both roles as you produce arguments that can be shared on the web.

Before we analyze some examples of argument in digital spaces, then, we offer a heuristic for teaching students to be MINDFUL readers and writers in social media spaces. (See Table 6.1.)

Table 6.1 Being a MINDFUL Reader and Writer of Social Media Arguments

	Action	As a reader of arguments made with social media (Consuming digital texts)	As a writer of arguments made with social media (Producing digital texts)
M	MONITOR your reading and writing	• What is your purpose for reading this message? • Who is the intended audience? What do you know about the other readers who would typically encounter this text? • Do you know and trust the writers in this network as peers, colleagues, and/or authorities?	• What is your purpose for composing this message? • Why have you chosen this particular medium (alphabetic text, meme, video, image)? • Are you simply reposting something that someone else produced without elaboration, commenting on something that someone else has produced, or sharing something that you created?
I	IDENTIFY the claim	• What is the main claim in this digital text? • What does the author/creator imply by stating this information? • Does the author explicitly make a claim, or make one implicitly simply by sharing it through social media?	• With your own digital writing, what is your main point? Have you made it clear? • When sharing the digital writing of others, have you elaborated on the author's/creator's claim, or just shared an original text without commentary or qualification? • How will your claim affect your intended audience? • How might your claim affect other, incidental audiences?
N	NOTE the evidence	• Does the author/creator provide evidence to support the claim being made? • What kind of evidence is used to support the claim—quotes from experts or noted individuals? Statistics? Anecdotes? • If an image is included in the message (or is the entire message), how is the evidence presented using effective visual design? How does the design affect your comprehension?	• What kind of evidence have you provided to support your claim? • Do you need to provide any links to sources? • If creating an image or video, have you considered the visual design aspects of your evidence?

continues

Table 6.1 Being a MINDFUL Reader and Writer of Social Media Arguments (*continued*)

	Action	As a reader of arguments made with social media (Consuming digital texts)	As a writer of arguments made with social media (Producing digital texts)
D	DETERMINE the framework and the mindset	• Does the evidence connect clearly to the claim? Is it warranted? • How are the author's/creator's beliefs, politics, and personal experiences used as a framework for interpretation? • Does the author's/creator's mind-set reinforce your preexisting notions, or does it make you think differently? Why?	• Will your intended audience question the warrants that connect your evidence to your claim? • Will an unintended audience question the warrants that connect your evidence to your claim? • How might you be guilty of "confirmation bias" (not considering additional evidence or other points of view)?
F	FACTS	• Does the author present facts, opinions, or both? • At a quick glance, does the data (times, dates, people involved, statistics, poll results, quotations) appear to be accurate and reliable? • Could this evidence be verified as fact by multiple sources? Have you checked to make sure?	• Have you verified your data as fact to bolster your own credibility and prepare for counterarguments? • Could the evidence you use be verified as fact by multiple sources?
U	UNDERSTAND the counter-argument	• What might other readers say in response to this argument? Is it fair? • Does the author/creator acknowledge other views? • Is the tone of the language civil or confrontational? • Also, do images, fonts, colors, and other visual aspects contribute to a civil or confrontational tone?	• Would readers outside of your target audience have a different opinion? • Would they question the reliability of the facts? • Do you need to offer a rebuttal? • Have you employed visual elements that differentiate your argument from the counterargument?
L	LEVERAGE your response	• What will your sharing of this information mean to readers in this network? • What does your endorsement mean? • Do you need to qualify the claim being made? • How might you call for (or engage in) further action?	

In addition, we call attention to the F (Facts) in the MINDFUL acronym because the emergent body of research cited above (e.g., Pariser; Vicario; World Economic Forum) tells us that sharing misinformation is a societal problem. There are many sites that help fact-check, find context for various issues, and gather data from nonpartisan sources. These are not "think tanks," which take distinctly partisan approaches, though we are sure that some people would take issue even with this list. Still, we need to teach students how to start with some resources that are ostensibly neutral, and we have listed a few in Table 6.2.

Table 6.2 Sites for Checking Facts and Finding Context for Issues

Sites for Checking Facts	Sites for Finding Context for Various Issues
• "[A] completely independent, self-sufficient entity wholly owned by its operators and funded through advertising revenues," Snopes: www.snopes.com/ • A project of the *Tampa Bay Times* and its partner news organizations, PolitiFact: www.politifact.com/ • A Project of the Annenberg Public Policy Center, FactCheck.org: www.factcheck.org/ • Center for Media and Democracy's Source Watch: www.sourcewatch.org/ • Center for Responsive Politics' Open Secrets: www.opensecrets.org/	• ProCon.org: www.procon.org/ • *The New York Times* Room for Debate: www.nytimes.com/roomfordebate • Pew Research: www.pewresearch.org/ • ProPublica: www.propublica.org/ • Document Cloud, "Search thousands of public documents from newsrooms across the country": www.documentcloud.org/home • The Center for Public Integrity, "Our mission: To serve democracy by revealing abuses of power, corruption and betrayal of public trust by powerful public and private institutions, using the tools of investigative journalism": www.publicintegrity.org/

Another useful resource is the "verification process and checklist" developed by journalists and other verification experts. *The Verification Handbook: A Definitive Guide to Verifying Digital Content for Emergency Coverage* (Silverman 2016) identifies a process for verifying user-generated content. Steve Buttry (2014) simplifies the process to a single mantra: "The question at the heart of verification is: 'How do you know that?'" He notes that journalists are supposed to "challenge" and "triangulate" facts from multiple sources, and an author's ability to do so includes three main factors:

1. A person's resourcefulness, persistence, skepticism, and skill

2. Sources' knowledge, reliability, and honesty, and the number, variety, and reliability of sources the writer can find and persuade to talk

3. Documentation

He suggests that technology, especially social media, is not an answer to a journalist's need to do research. Instead, he wonders how "[w]e can use new tools most effectively by employing them with those old questions: How do they know that? How else do they know that?" For additional insights on this process of verification, we suggest the weekly program *On the Media*, a show produced by National Public Radio's WNYC, and its continuing series called the "Breaking News Consumer's Handbook." Here, one can find context that is useful for thinking about news stories related to various topics such as natural disasters, health epidemics, and political matters. Additionally, *On the Media*'s free, downloadable "Breaking News Consumer's Handbook" PDF (www.wnyc.org/story/breaking-news-consumers-handbook -pdf/) offers a succinct list of points to help listeners, viewers, and readers critically consider news coverage in the wake of a major media event.

Finally, if a website looks suspicious, a WHOIS query can yield some interesting results. An internet protocol, much like HTTP or FTP for websites, or IMAP, POP, and TCP for email, users can initiate a WHOIS search using a site like Domain Tools. This particular site will show quick stats on any domain including the country of origin, the IP history, a contact email address, and will also provide screenshot history. If this investigation still does not yield useful results, a trip to the Internet Archive's WayBack Machine can be useful, too. This site captures snapshots of countless domains, some dating back to the very beginning of the visual web in 1996. While these tools may not result in finding every fraud, they could be useful.

In short, we know that social media is—by its very nature—a place where ideas and emotions are shared quickly, sometimes without much forethought, and certainly not in a vacuum. Still, we can help our students, especially in middle and high school, to develop the socio–emotional skills that they need to communicate with peers and the broader public while, at the same time, learning how to make logical arguments. If we fail to bring social media—and the ways in which it invites and allows for robust, intellectual arguments that move beyond petty chatter—into a conversation with our students, we are doing them a disservice.

Developing Arguments via Social Media

To build students' mindfulness in social media spaces, we first need to help them see their participation in those networks as *real* reading and writing. This feat requires us to rethink the kinds of texts we ask our students to read and to write and the way we value their out-of-school literacies in the classroom. The following gateway activity ("Finding Arguments in My Social-Reading Life"), adapted from one of the general reading lessons in our book *Connected Reading: Teaching Adolescent Readers in a Digital World* (2015), helps students to metacognitively think about their reading practices and practice seeing social media as a reading and writing space.

Gateway Activity: Finding Arguments in My Social-Reading Life

Weeklong Reflection: This week we will be focusing on the reading that you do on a daily basis—in your social media networks. You will work with a partner to investigate how people argue in these networks. What kinds of claims do they make? How do they respond when they don't agree with something that is said? You will collect data early in the week, and at the end of the week you will share the results of your investigation.

Day 1: Identify the networks where you, your partner, your peers, and adults in your lives read. Consider Instagram, Facebook, Twitter, gaming communities, and other digital spaces. Select several sample posts from different networks to analyze. Try to collect a variety of posts that range from short to long, from text-based to image-based, and from having many comments to few or none.

Day 2: Uncover the hidden arguments. Read through the sample posts and start to form a hypothesis about how people make claims, respond to claims, and provide evidence for what they say. What are the hidden (or not so hidden) ways people argue, debate, and discuss issues?

Day 3: Reflect on how people make arguments in these networks. Do you see the same argument techniques within a particular network? Across networks? Which techniques seem to be the most effective?

Days 4 and 5: Share the results of your inquiry, and listen to your peers as they share their results. As a class, develop a list of observations. Then consider what you've learned about reading posts in your social network. Make a list of tips to help other students your age see and understand the arguments embedded in social media.

Once students are able to identify arguments in social media, we can ask them to engage in mindful arguing via social media. The weekly "Do Now" activity from KQED that we discussed earlier in the chapter provides some real-world opportunities to do just that. (See ww2.kqed.org/education/about-do-now/.) Dawn Reed (@dawnreed), a high school English teacher in Okemos, Michigan, uses the prompts—which include at least one multimedia text, a short article with additional links and resources, and several options for "Do Next" tasks—to periodically engage her students in argument through social media.

For instance, in the fall of 2015, KQED's "Do Now" featured a story from PBS' *NewsHour* Extra, "Has Standardized Testing in the U.S. Gone Too Far?" and invited students to share their ideas with the #DoNowTesting hashtag. Because Dawn's school blocks Twitter from student use, her students focus on blog comments and their interactions are limited to other bloggers.

Nearly every comment—from students around the country—on this post took the form of a direct response to the original story. In traditional terms, we would identify it as "call and response." For instance, one of Dawn's students wrote the following:

> *Some tests being given to students nowadays are unnecessary. The tests given along with coursework in schools should be enough to give an accurate placement of the students. If a test is not necessary to get into college then it should not be required in high school either. High school is preparation for college and giving students more stress by requiring more tests will not help their overall performance. If anything the tests could be an option for the students who want to check their knowledge, but they should not be required.*

Though the responders had the opportunity to reply to each other, nearly all of them stayed focused on the initial prompt. This kind of writing in and of itself is useful in that it helps students to think about a current topic and begin to develop a reasoned opinion. The next step is to get students interacting with each other as they test, defend, and refine their thinking, something Dawn encourages her students to do by replying to other commenters. Though her students couldn't participate, many others could, and this kind of conversation is exactly what happened as the #DoNowTesting hashtag exploded on Twitter.

We checked the Twitter conversation to see how students were engaging in argument. The first thing we noticed was that they were using multiple modes to participate. For instance, one student, R, joined the conversation by posting the image shown in Figure 6.3 in response to another person's tweet. By creating and posting this meme, the student claimed that tests can be frustrating, giving evidence to support that claim that some teachers give tests on things that haven't been taught. In turn, like the woman featured in the image, it can bring a student to tears, full of frustration and stress. As the conversation continued, another student, E, replied directly to this claim. He took the stance that testing is, in fact, useful: "Testing is the best way to review on what we have learned."

Immediately after, A replied, "I agree with you for me it's just like a review and useful." This same student, utilizing one of the more recent additions to the features of Twitter, posted a poll in order to collect data on the question inspired by R's

Figure 6.3 Testing Meme

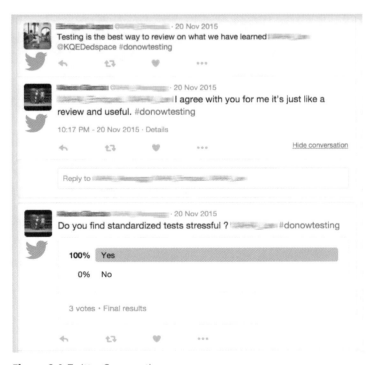

Figure 6.4 Twitter Conversation

meme: "Do you find standardized tests stressful?" Three people completed her poll, showing a unanimous "yes."

At this point, E shifted his position, perhaps swayed by the evidence being presented in the conversation, stating, "Standardized tests are a[n] unnecessary weight in [sic] student backs and backpacks." He paired this claim with a political cartoon showcasing stressed-out administrators, teachers, and, bearing the brunt of it all, students.

E was not the only person to shift his position during the conversation. It seemed that as more students presented data in response to counterarguments, many students changed views. This powerful possibility in social networking—to persuade others—has been realized in social and political movements around the world. When students can see this power at work and identify the argumentative moves that social media writers make to effect change, they can consume social media without being so readily affected by them, and they can use argumentative strategies in their own digital writing.

Social media can be the civic forum that it was once promised to be, so long as we teach students how to read, write, and participate in thoughtful, engaging ways. Writing-by-the-way helps them to gather data, try out ideas, and respond to counters. Through written conversation, the students can revise their overall arguments in response to feedback. Using social media, they are able to promote their ideas and push back against others.

Practical Matters: How Does a Writer Attend to Issues of Citation, Plagiarism, and Fair Use When Crafting Social Media?

Now that we have explored issues of copyright and fair use (Chapter 3), citation formats and reasonable adaptations for digital writing (Chapter 4), and copyleft sources (Chapter 5), in this section we discuss these issues with one particular form of digital media: images. Images pose a special set of opportunities for us as digital readers and writers. Consider how R's post in Figure 6.3 used an image to make its most powerful claims. Unfortunately, images also pose a special set of problems. For instance:

- It is becoming more common for students to include images in their writing, both print and digital. Usually, these are taken from outside sources and not created by the writer. At this level, the issue of accurate citation becomes important.

- While there are a number of ways to quickly search the web for images, attributing those images to the original creator can often be challenging, especially if an image is popular and has been embedded in a number of websites. Here, attribution is even more important, especially if the image will be repurposed.

- Finally, even if an original image is found, there's a good chance that the student has somehow repurposed the image. An intentional remix— which might include color alteration, zooming, cropping, copying and pasting all or part of the image into another, or other editorial changes— is one way an image could be manipulated. Thus, any effort at accurate attribution becomes even more complicated by the collaborative process.

As an illustration, let's explore one image that Troy had to research in order to find an accurate citation for this chapter. The image in question came from Jake's poster, the silhouette of the woman with the megaphone paired with the sentence "Inspire the CHANGE you want to see in the world" (Figure 6.5). To find the original

Figure 6.5 Taking a Screenshot of Jake's digital poster
Kid with Megaphone © 2013 by Maya Gonzalez, Reflection Press. All rights reserved.

Figure 6.6 Google Image Search Interface

source of the image, Troy first took a snapshot of just the woman with the megaphone using TechSmith's Snagit software (though there are many free alternatives that can be used for the snapshot feature).

Then he navigated to https://images.google.com and clicked on the "Upload an Image" option, choosing his screenshot from his saved files (Figure 6.6).

Google yielded its search results for "campaign megaphone" (Figure 6.7).

Figure 6.7 Google Image Search Result

Finally, clicking on the image brought up the full search for this image. To view the image in context, Troy had to do some clicking around on the individual images to see additional information about each item, though they all looked the same. This would bring up an additional subsearch on the Google page showing the original image with the option of either visiting the page on which it was found or viewing the image as a separate file. Troy searched through the first few versions of the image, exploring different web pages where it had been used (Figure 6.8).

Figure 6.8 Google Image Search Result for Individual Photo
Kid with Megaphone © 2013 by Maya Gonzalez, Reflection Press. All rights reserved.

To the best of his ability, he determined that the first instance of this particular image came in 2013 on a blog called *Reflection Press*, which ultimately led to the citation included in this chapter. While it is impossible to know for sure exactly where this clip art silhouette originated, Troy conducted due diligence to try and find the original source.

It is through this process of identifying specific images, searching for the original source, and then citing those sources that we can help students delve more deeply into finding accurate citations. While it is not foolproof, it is at least a step in the right direction. Asking students to do a digital forensic analysis of a photo that they might use (if the original attribution source is not easily attainable) reminds them that, even if that photo is on the Internet, someone created the original image file. Consequently, to the best of our ability, we should try to identify the original source. This process speaks to the academic expectations of accurate citation.

Taking It to the Classroom

We close this group of chapters on reading and writing digital arguments—on social media, blog posts, infographics, and videos—by sharing some insights from teacher and edublogger Katharine Hale (@KatharineHale). On her blog, *TEaCHitivity*, Katharine writes about the many ways that she and her students use digital reading and writing in a workshop environment. In January 2016, she shared a post entitled "Branding Student Writing." While she was alluding specifically to blogging, her advice applies to any form of digital writing:

> *I challenge you to rethink how you use blogs in your classroom. Let go of the weekly prompts or the writing assignments. Instead, spend a long week helping students develop their brand. Help them list potential topics and then push them to double check that their topic is sustainable by creating a list of 5 blog posts they could already write in relation to that topic. A good brand takes time. (Hale 2016)*

Also, she pushes our thinking more by suggesting that

> *[branding] is definitely different than what we have been taught to do as writing teachers. We are taught to inspire students to write by giving them lots of writing themes or ideas. Unfortunately, no matter how brilliant our writing topics are, our topics are ours, not theirs. We must teach students how to find their own writing topics by sifting through their own life and their own stories.*

Katharine's overarching idea—that we need to inspire writers to develop their own ideas—is one that has been echoing through conversations about teaching writing for decades. From our origins with Don Murray and Don Graves all the way to the present generation, including Katharine as well as Kristin Ziemke, Katie Muhtaris, Allison Marchetti, and Rebekah O'Dell, we hear similar calls to action. The new layer that these contemporary voices add is that digital writing can bring students incredible new opportunities for personal investment, sustained interest, and a lifelong habit of writing.

Social media, then, must be embraced as a form of reading and writing. By helping our students to be MINDFUL, we can shift their participation. Here are a few more ideas to get started with this work:

- Print out or snapshot the comments in one thread of a news article or blog. Have students trace the argument through annotations. Who makes a claim? Who provides evidence? Who counters? After annotating, students can adopt the roles of individuals they read in the discussion and hold the conversation in the classroom. In a fishbowl setting, the rest of the class can critique the arguments being made, calling for more evidence, attention to rebuttals, etc.

Figure 6.9 THINK Acronym

- Millicent Roskie works with students in grades 3–5 in New Jersey as a technology teacher. She knows how important their online footprints will be in the future, so she introduces them to a version of the MINDFUL approach described earlier. In Milli's classes—reinforced by a prominently displayed bulletin board in the school hallway—students must THINK (Milli downloaded this graphic, created by Shannon at www.technologyrocksseriously.com for the board). See Figure 6.9.

  Though she works with younger students, Milli introduces them to some of the social networks that they will (or already) encounter, and she encourages them to build positive digital footprints. By asking them to pause and THINK before composing, even if only on their Google Classroom forum, she is asking them to be mindful about their reading and writing in social media.

- Beth Grasso, a middle school guidance counselor, guides the peer leaders in her school to talk to younger students about their social media lives. The students themselves had identified the problem of "chasing likes," so Beth had the group design a lesson called "It's (not) about the 'likes.'" This idea can be used in any classroom by having students discuss what it means to "like" something on social media and how they themselves are influenced by "chasing likes." Small groups can create PSAs or other digital presentations that argue for individuals to focus on sparking conversation with their posts, as compared to searching for "likes."

- Eighth-grade teacher Laura Garrison takes social media offline by creating a space on the wall for students to post "status updates" where they can share ideas or articles they have read—and respond to each other. By turning the bulletin board into a "social media wall," the students have visible opportunities to reflect on their contributions. After a few days of contributing, Laura has them look at the wall together to talk about "extending the conversation." By giving students time to read what has been written and then to discuss the posts that contributed versus those that were "pointless," Laura asks them to think critically about what they posted on the wall for all to see. She challenges them to take this lesson to their social media lives and to extend the conversation in positive ways.

CHAPTER 7

COACHING STUDENTS' WORK WITH DIGITAL ARGUMENTS

Coaching Students as They Read and Write Digital Arguments

In his book *Write for Insight: Empowering Content Area Learning, Grades 6–12*, William Strong (2006) says, "When it comes to writing, we can serve either as **coaches** or as **judges**" (emphasis in original, p. 130). He makes the case that writing teachers should act as coaches for students as they develop their writing, responding with instructional support much like athletic coaches, who identify player weaknesses and help them to practice the skills needed to gain expertise. Judging, Strong argues, comes with grading, when writing teachers evaluate the quality of a product against certain criteria. Students learn to write during moments of coaching and practice, not by viewing evaluative comments or rubric scores.

As teachers, we can all think of instances when Strong's insights have proven to be true in our own writing (and reading!) classrooms, and perhaps even in our own experiences as students. Even if we have never used the terms *coach* or *judge* to categorize our roles in teaching literacy, we've looked for ways to encourage students and build on their strengths rather than simply evaluate their work. We've also built our own repertoires of moves for providing feedback and guidance, such as conferencing, responding to annotations or drafts, or facilitating peer feedback experiences. But what happens when the texts that students are considering or constructing aren't static? How does one leave marginal notes in a video or ask students to annotate when they're reading a web-based text? In this chapter, we'll explore methods for using formative assessment to coach students when they're working on-screen and online, with multimedia texts that employ digital argument.

Coaching Through Formative Assessment

Embedded within earlier chapters are examples of how to assess students' learning and use their work to inform our instruction. For instance, in Chapter 3 we examined Khadi's blog post, noting which strategies and features of blogs she used effectively and identifying areas where we could focus instruction for her (and her classmates) in the future. This kind of assessment and reflective practice lies at the heart of our teaching, and in this section we will focus explicitly on assessment of students' work—both their processes and their products—as a means of coaching students to deeper argumentative thinking.

We know that assessment is an important topic, yet we want to be clear: this chapter will not provide a set of rubrics to grade students. In fact, we will mention grading only because we know that at some point teachers likely have to quantify the work students are doing into a grade, simply because that is the educational system in which we work. Many other scholars and teachers, notably Alfie Kohn (www.AlfieKohn.org) , have presented much more elaborate and detailed critiques of grades and grading and the ways in which they destroy genuine inquiry and learning.

While it may seem like we are shirking our responsibility here by ignoring grades in a final chapter about assessment (and it is a topic that we often encounter in our work with teachers), we see grades as a function of *evaluation*, and we respectfully defer to you to decide how, ultimately, to evaluate your students' work in terms of grades, points, and other markers that show how well they are performing along a scale of quality.

That said, we believe assessment is critically important. Because we do not equate "grading" with assessment, our focus here will be on revealing how you can see your students' developing prowess in argumentative thinking and how you might respond to them in order to push them further.

Are We Assessing Declarative or Procedural Knowledge? Form or Substance?

In the opening pages of *Assessing Students' Digital Writing: Protocols for Looking Closely*, Troy tried to capture the challenge that we face with assessment of writing in our modern age.

> We understand that both the processes and products of writing continue to undergo change in the digital age; thus, it is crucial that teachers at all grade levels begin to initiate serious conversations about how writing is taught, how we value the process of writing, and how we pay attention to the assessments of students' multimodal compositions. (2015, p. 2)

We also know that readers of these new kinds of digital texts must develop knowledge of the features so that they can employ strategies to read critically, and we must assess these reading skills. So what does this mean for teaching arguments in digital spaces? Let's return for a minute to our inquiry cube (Figure 7.1), described in Chapter 1, p. 12.

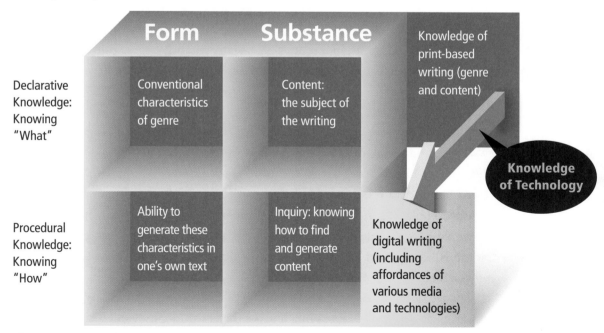

Figure 7.1 Inquiry Cube

Adapted from Hicks, T., K. H. Turner, and J. Stratton. 2013. "Reimagining a Writer's Process Through Digital Storytelling." *LEARNing Landscapes* 6 (2): 167–183.

Declarative knowledge represents *what* a student knows about a given text. Teachers can use the strategies in this book to help students identify the features for many types of digital argument: blogs and other web-based texts, infographics, videos, and social media (*declarative knowledge of form*). Additionally, all arguments—including digital arguments—must have claims supported by warranted evidence, and should attend to counterarguments when necessary (*declarative knowledge of substance*).

However, as we and others (such as George Hillocks 1995, 2011) have argued, declarative knowledge is not enough. While it is important for students to understand the features of arguments in general, and digital arguments in particular, they must also be able to critically deconstruct them as readers and produce them as writers. To that end, we must help them develop procedural knowledge—or the actual doing—of both substance and form.

Yet, as our cube indicates, we believe that the craft of digital argument blurs the lines around procedural knowledge. As we have shown throughout the book, with even the smallest change in font choice, color selection, or hyperlink placement, students need to be mindful of how the technology allows them to shape both form and substance. In turn, as readers of these texts, students need to understand all the possible moves digital writers could have used, as well as their actual writing moves. Procedural knowledge, then, requires that we constantly assess our students and provide them with feedback that coaches them to deeper argumentative thinking.

Assessing Knowledge of Form

In earlier chapters, we provide tables that list the basic features of blogs, infographics, videos, and social media. These lists answer the question: "What does this form of writing look like?" Some of these features are the kinds of things we have assessed in writing for decades. For example, blogs are often written in concise paragraphs made of complete sentences, syntactic features that teachers fifty or a hundred years ago would have found valuable as well. Blogs are relatively new, yes, but the more traditional elements of writing that exist within digital texts still need to be coached and assessed.

As we noted in earlier chapters, there is another important consideration for evaluating students' digital reading and writing: born digital texts include features that printed texts do not. For instance, blogs use digital media and hyperlinks to further the argument, and we want students to use such features in their writing and recognize them in their reading. To assess a student's knowledge of form, then, we can create checklists of these features (see Table 7.1 for a sample checklist).

However, these kinds of lists can become required criteria for students' writing. As we have seen in the vibrant examples of students' work with digital argument in this book, these arguments are never as simple as inserting a hyperlink or image or organizing ideas through bulleted lists. As we noted in our article "No Longer a Luxury: Digital Literacy Can't Wait":

> *Setting a minimum number of slides, images, transitions, links, or other*
> *digital elements in student projects does little to improve digital literacy. In*
> *much the same way that some of the most reductive writing pedagogy has*
> *created patterns (five paragraphs of five sentences each, for instance), we now*
> *see similar trends happening with slide shows, websites, digital stories, and*

Table 7.1 Sample Checklist for Assessment of Knowledge of Form

Does this blog post indicate that the student understands the following features of a blog?	
• Contains roughly 250–1,000 words	_____
• Employs a first-person point of view	_____
• Includes links to outside resources, including news items, other blog posts, or various media	_____
• Develops with short paragraphs that are aesthetically pleasing and functional for reading	_____
• Utilizes additional text features such as images, subheadings, bulleted lists, and other informational text features	_____

other types of digital writing projects. Rather than focusing on content—and developing an appropriate message—the assignments focus on the most basic elements of form: the things that can be counted. (2013, p. 60)

In reading and writing digital arguments—just as in *all* reading and writing—students need to make choices based on their purpose, the work's context, and the work's audience. Though our lists of features may be helpful reminders when considered flexibly, using them as checklists for assessment can result in an artificial kind of reading and writing that won't help students to work with digital arguments in the real world.

It is one thing to assess whether a student can identify or produce the form of a particular kind of writing; most important, though, we want to assess their thinking as they read or write. Therefore, we now turn our attention to how we can capture students' thinking as they read and gauge their ability to produce various arguments. In our view, having students reflect on their reading and writing is the primary way to assess these areas. To that end, we will describe three teachers who assess students' argument thinking through formative assessment and student reflection, all the while using these assessments to coach students to improved reading and writing of digital arguments.

Helping Students to Focus with Learning Targets

Let's return to Lauren's class—the students we met in Chapter 5 who were crafting public service announcements about topics that they found socially compelling. Lauren's school practices standards-based grading, which means students are evaluated on learning targets throughout the marking period. During the PSA unit, Lauren coaches her students to meet the learning targets outlined in Table 7.2.

When we take a close look at these criteria, we notice that the first three targets—all focused on constructing a researched argument—resemble criteria we might include in a rubric for a traditional essay. Clearly, Lauren values the intentionality and efficacy of the students' arguments, and she is looking for student growth in those areas rather than checking for an arbitrary number of video techniques or pieces of evidence. The final target also requires Lauren to assess her students throughout their process. She takes into account her formative assessment as they complete "drafts"—in this case a storyboard and script—and considers students' use of feedback to achieve the final product.

Table 7.2 Criteria for Mastering Learning Targets in Lauren's PSA Unit

Learning Target	To Achieve Mastery Level
I can develop a claim and support it with relevant evidence.	• Claim is precise and completely addresses the task. • Claim is supported throughout with evidence and reasoning. • Claim acknowledges the audience's knowledge level and explains the general context.
I can develop a valid counterclaim to strengthen my own claim.	• Includes valid reasoning and evidence for counterclaim. • Logically sequences claim, counterclaim, reason, and evidence. • Sufficiently explains the limitations of the counterclaim. • May use sentence starters to explain the counterclaim.
I can effectively document research collected from a variety of sources.	• Gathers relevant information from multiple sources. • Conducts independent research with assistance from peers and/or teacher. • Includes evidence from a variety of sources. • Correctly formats MLA in-text citations and bibliography.
I can use the writing process to produce a professional video.	• Writing product shows awareness of the task, purpose, and audience. • One or more drafts exist, showing evidence of planning, revision, and editing. • Utilizes feedback to revise and improve writing. • "Director's cut" clearly explains compositional choices. • All elements of writing process are complete (demonstrates writing stamina).

The targets give Lauren a clear idea of what to look for in her students' work. More importantly, sharing learning targets with students when they embark on a project helps them to understand and own the skills involved in doing this work.

Because their final products would take the form of video, Lauren encouraged the groups to include images and video clips in addition to quotations or statistics that could be presented on the screen in text form. As she conferenced with Jothan and Anthony about their storyboard, Lauren commended them on their plan to video themselves conversing about a friend who had been raped. The script revealed the story of one girl, told from the perspective of two male friends who were hoping that she would report the crime. Lauren quickly realized that the argument lacked focus—a requirement of the first learning target in the list above. She could not pinpoint their primary claim, and she did not see any evidence beyond the personal anecdote.

During the conference, she asked the pair, "What point are you trying to make?" They were able to clarify that they wanted to make the claim that rapes are a problem among teen girls, and they should be reported. Lauren worked with the students to consider how they might bolster the personal anecdote with some statistics to help make their case. Jothan and Anthony's final video cut between the live shots of the two boys telling the story of their female friend and screens showing national statistics (see Figure 7.2).

Figure 7.2 Screenshots from Jothan and Anthony's PSA

Jothan and Anthony highlighted the statistical evidence by overlaying the type on a black screen, thus drawing a stark contrast between the anecdote and the statistics. Lauren's formative assessment of the storyboard and script against the learning targets helped her to guide her students' thinking about their argument. She helped them articulate the ways that the evidence tied to the claim and how, using a strong visual clue, they could make that evidence more prominent for viewers.

Reflecting with Google Forms

Valerie Mattessich (@VMattPV), a high school teacher in northeastern New Jersey, asks students in her English classes to create book trailers that make arguments about books they have read. She prepares them for this task through activities that focus on understanding the role images can play in their digital videos.

Because she is concerned with their developing abilities in reading and writing arguments, her primary assessment of the task is through a reflection that the students complete after they have produced their own book trailers and viewed some of their classmates' work. She asks two simple questions, and collects student responses via Google Forms (see Figure 7.3):

1. Please discuss what aspects of argumentation you learned from completing this project (your own trailer).

2. Please discuss what knowledge of argumentation you gained by watching and analyzing the trailers of others.

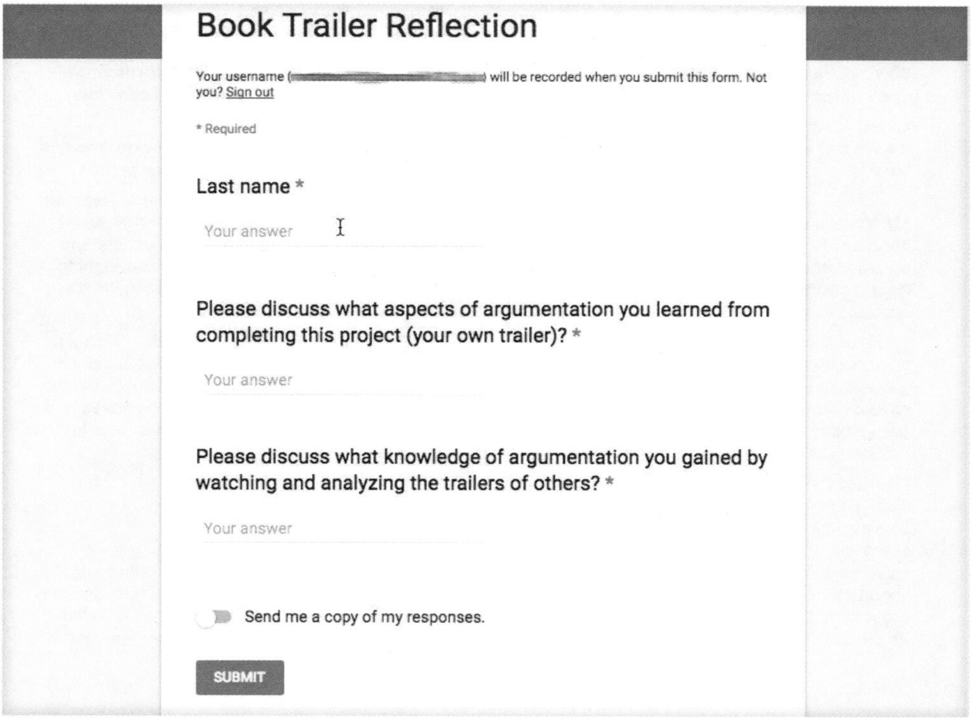

Figure 7.3 Val's Google Form

By collecting the responses in a form, Val is able to consider particular students individually as well as look collectively, across the group, to see patterns of student strengths and weaknesses. For instance, as she scrolled through the responses (see Figure 7.4), she noticed that most students commented on Aristotelian appeals, which was something the class had been working on, and only a few specifically

	D	E
1	Please discuss what aspects of argumentation you learned from completing this project (your own trailer)?	Please discuss what knowledge of argumentation you gained by watching and analyzing the trailers of others?
5	I learned more about appeals and how even though unconsciously you don't think about them they are almost always used.	I learned that each book can be interpreted in a different way depending on your perspective. Where I saw a good pathos appeal approach others took a ethos appeal instead. This isn't bad its just interesting to see what perspective people can have on the same things.
6	How to show the theme of the story but not give too much away or don't show the right perspective of a certain character.	How the effects of music and text can really impact how you see the story and how so much thought goes behind producing a trailer or advertisement.
7	I learned the difference between logos, pathos, and ethos and was able to use them to help my classmates understand my book.	I learned the different ways the 3 Aristotelian appeals can be interpreted with different stories.
8	I learned that when creating any work, you don't really plan around your appeals. If you're doing something well they just sort of happen. They are often subtle and takes a keen eye to distinguish one from another.	I gained a better process of determining appeals when presented to me. Instead of just thinking "that was good/bad" now I can have a fuller and more complete way of analyzing any sort of media that I consume.
9	I learned more about the pathos appeal and how trailers can affect people's emotions and draw them in	I learned about the ethos appeal and how reviews and people's culture can be a way to convince people
10	My creating my own trailer, I learned that it is important to get straight to the point when forming an argument. Since the trailer was short, I had to clearly incorporate my claim as well as use ethos, pathos, or logos to support it.	By watching and analyzing trailers of others, I learned how to pick up on which appeals they used to reveal their claim. Some claims were harder to understand than others, therefore I learned that it is important to make not allow your support to deviate from the claim itself.
11	When arguing there will most likely be a strong point of pathos. You also want to make sure that you know enough about the subject that you can have a conversation about it and if thrown a curve ball you can deflect it. You want to be able to support whatever it is that you're representing.	I learned that when creating an argument or idea you want to make sure you can portray to your audience the basic idea of what you're saying without giving too much away. You want to keep the person hooked and leave them wondering what else there is to your idea or, in this case, book.
12	I learned that audio plays a huge part in your claim and can strengthen what you are trying to convey. I also learned that with just the tweaking of the way you present your visuals, your trailer could mean something else entirely and it is important to make sure that your elements of argumentation (ethos, logos, pathos) are evident for the viewer.	I learned that some people are better at conveying the elements of argumentation better than others, and the trailers that appeared more impactful often included good use of audio, visual, and Aristotelian elements.

Figure 7.4 Responses from Students via Google Forms

mentioned claim or how audio and image can affect the argument. This assessment allowed Val to plan instruction focused specifically on the role of media (audio and image) in crafting a digital argument.

Learning from Peers with Social Annotation

When reading is isolated to print-based texts, the idea of social annotation is, well, unimaginable. The words that we write in the margin or on a sticky note are maintained only in our own version of the book. Digital texts, however, are networked, and a variety of tools enable readers to interact *during* reading of online texts. As of this printing, tools such as Ponder, Genius, and Hypothes.is are helping people to comment on (and share comments on) online content.

In Sara Kajder's (@skajder) eighth-grade class in Georgia, her students use Hypothes.is to collaboratively think about texts. As she peruses the "think marks" of her individual students—and their responses to each other—she is able to see their argumentative thinking on her screen. For example, as Sara reviewed the student annotations on an article related to climate change, she noticed the following:

> **Student comment:**   This is legit.
> **Peer response:**   Do better for us. Support and describe why.

She was pleased to see the second student pushing the first to support his comment. It showed her that this student understood the need for evidence. Similarly, in the next example, she noticed the peer asking for deeper argumentative thinking.

> **Student comment:**   Yup.
> **Peer response:**   You know you don't get to make that play. Give us more, son.

Because she saw a trend among her students to offer initial comments that did not fully critique the argument in the text, Sara used both of these responses in a minilesson the next day that focused on identifying and responding to claims within the text. She asked her students to return to the text and annotate with this focus; they then logged their work in their digital reading notebooks, where she gave them individual feedback. Because these annotations were social, she was able to see deeper levels of understanding as the students responded to each other's comments.

Listening to Students' Thinking with Screencasting and Screen Captures

We are often asked what tool we would pick for our classroom if we had to limit ourselves to one. Though we admit that this is a hard choice, we think our assessment practices have been most transformed by screencasting and screen capture tools.

Screencasting

Have you ever looked at a piece of student work after school and wished that the student were sitting next to you so that she could help you better understand her intent or the choices she made? Screencasts—video recordings of what's happening on a computer screen, with accompanying narration—give students an opportunity to talk through their process and to clarify their intentions. As students think aloud during a screencast, we can see their motions on the screen and hear their thoughts about the text. While our goal is always to have students create digital work that can stand alone without explanatory commentary, screencasting is a powerful formative assessment tool that gives teachers a window into students' independent work and encourages student reflection.

Table 7.3 Screencasting Tools

Web-based	Screencast-O-Matic	https://screencast-o-matic.com/
	Screencastify (Google Chrome)	www.screencastify.com/
Computer programs	Jing (Mac and Windows)	www.techsmith.com/jing.html
	QuickTime (Mac)	https://support.apple.com/downloads/quicktime
	Camtasia (Mac and Windows)	www.techsmith.com/camtasia.html
Apps	Explain Everything	http://explaineverything.com/
	ShowMe	www.showme.com/
	Educreations	www.educreations.com/

In Jennifer Zito's ninth-grade class, her students used screencasts as they annotated passages from Sue Monk Kidd's *The Secret Life of Bees* (2003). The screencasts enabled Jen to assess students' comprehension and their ability to read closely, tracking not just what they said as they read, but also what passages they had noted, how they moved through the on-screen text, and how those notes helped them to develop an argument.

We can focus our formative assessment by giving students particular purposes or prompts for their screencasts. For instance, when reading a blog post, a student could record a screencast as a "think-aloud" where she describes the various text features and key passages, and how the images support the main idea. Alternatively, a student could record a screencast in which he provides a reflective response to one of his own projects. Clicking through various elements on-screen, he might recall the choices that he made as he developed a digital argument.

Screen capture

Screen capture tools allow users to, as the name implies, snap a picture of a screen and then annotate it with text, lines, circles, highlighting, or other features. Much like screencasting, a screen capture can be used by students to share their thinking about a reading or offer comments about their own writing. In contrast to a screencast from every student—which, even at a minute long, could take hours of viewing time by the teacher—a screen capture can clearly demonstrate a specific moment in the reading process or an element in a piece of digital writing.

Table 7.4 Screen Capture Tools

Web-based	Awesome Screenshot	www.awesomescreenshot.com/
	FireShot	http://getfireshot.com/
Computer programs	Jing (Mac and Windows)	www.techsmith.com/jing.html
	Monosnap (Mac and Windows)	http://monosnap.com/
	Preview (included with Mac OSX)	
	Camtasia (Mac and Windows)	www.techsmith.com/camtasia.html

For instance, in Figure 7.5, Troy has created a brief annotation on Khadi's blog post using the Mac's screenshot feature with Preview. He captured the image (Command + Shift + 4) and then opened it in Preview. He added a circle around one sentence, inserted a text box with a comment, and then drew an arrow between them. He could then share this screenshot with Khadi or embed it in a longer, textual response.

Similarly, he could have recorded a response to Khadi with screencasting tools, pointing to specific sections of the text, highlighting those sections, and scrolling through the entire blog post while offering comments.

Both screen capture and screencasting tools allow us to interact with our students and their writing asynchronously and with great specificity. They enable teachers and students to move beyond simply documenting declarative knowledge about form and substance. To help students to create their own screen captures and screencasts, reflecting on their work more deeply, consider the following prompts:

- As a reader, what worked well for you in this digital argument? What did the author accomplish through the use of text, images, sounds, and other media? Where did you struggle to make meaning from this text? Ultimately, do you agree with the claim?

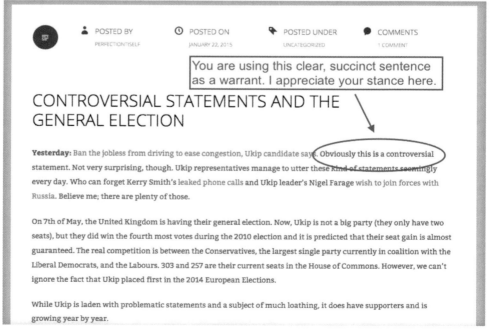

Figure 7.5 Annotation of Khadi's Blog Post

- As a writer, discuss the ways in which you composed your digital argument. What is your overall claim, and what kinds of evidence did you use to support it? In what ways did you blend text, images, sounds, and other media in a logical, rhetorically sophisticated manner?

- As a reader, how did a particular element of digital writing produce a desired effect?

- As a writer, how did you craft digital writing to have a desired effect on your readers?

Conclusion

In closing, we return to the question that we posed at the end of Chapter 1: Why teach digital arguments? While there are many answers to that question throughout the book, we want to end with one that cuts to the heart of the matter for us. As teachers and teacher educators, helping students at all age levels and capabilities to become better readers and writers is part of our DNA. Teaching, quite simply, is what we do.

Yet at another level, we have had many conversations about digital literacy as parents. At the risk of making too broad of an emotional appeal—after all, we have tried to rely heavily on evidence throughout the book!—both of us answer the question of why we should teach digital arguments with an emphatic reply: *because our children's lives depend on it.* They must be able to critically analyze digital arguments created by others—from advertisers to academics, from their friends on social media to bloggers they will never meet in person. Moreover, our children must be able to enter conversations with multiple authors/producers of digital arguments by creating their own. Along with the goal of raising responsible kids, we genuinely hope that teaching digital arguments can change our civic discourse.

We look forward to continuing these conversations and hearing about your experiences in teaching digital argument on our wiki: http://argumentintherealworld.wikispaces.com/.

Works Cited

Andrews, RJ. 2014. "Creative Routines." Info We Trust, March 26. www.infowetrust.com/creative-routines/.

Belonwu, V. 2013. "The Absolutely Essential Components of an Eye-Catching, Informative Infographic." Business Gross, May 3. http://businessgross.com/2013/05/03/the-absolutely-essential-components-of-an-eye-catching-informative-infographic/.

Belshaw, D. 2012. "Beyond Elegant Consumption." *Open Educational Thinkering* (blog), March 30. http://dougbelshaw.com/blog/2012/03/30/beyond-elegant-consumption/.

Bhuller, G. 2014. "5 Key Elements of a Successful Infographic." Envisionup, January 17. www.envisionup.com/ask-the-envision-gurus/5-key-elements-of-a-successful-infographic/.

Buttry, S. 2014. "Verification Fundamentals: Rules to Live By." In *The Verification Handbook: A Definitive Guide to Verifying Digital Content for Emergency Coverage*, edited by C. Silverman (Chapter 2). http://verificationhandbook.com/book/chapter2.php.

Chen, A. 2016. "Stand to Work if You Like, but Don't Brag About the Benefits." NPR, March 17. www.npr.org/sections/health-shots/2016/03/17/470713717/stand-to-work-if-you-like-but-dont-brag-about-its-benefits.

Chowdhry, A. 2015. "Facebook Hoax: Mark Zuckerberg Is Not Giving Away $4.5 Million to 1,000 Users." *Forbes*, December 29. www.forbes.com/sites/amitchowdhry/2015/12/29/facebook-hoax-mark-zuckerberg-is-not-giving-away-4-5-million-to-1000-users/#3e0b5d985913/.

Cillizza, C. 2016. "Sarah Palin's Rambling, Remarkable and at Times Hard to Understand Endorsement of Donald Trump." *Washington Post*, January 20. www.washingtonpost.com/news/the-fix/wp/2016/01/20/sarah-palins-rambling-remarkable-and-at-times-hard-to-understand-endorsement-of-donald-trump/.

Coca-Cola. 2014. "It's Beautiful." Super Bowl commercial (video file). www.youtube.com/watch?v=ry6aFSK6UEk.

Copyright Confusion. "Reasoning: How Do I Know if My Use Is a Fair Use?" 2016. http://copyrightconfusion.wikispaces.com/Reasoning.

Daniels, H., and S. Ahmed. 2014. *Upstanders: How to Engage Middle School Hearts and Minds with Inquiry*. Portsmouth, NH: Heinemann.

Daudova, K. 2015. "Controversial Statements and the General Election." *Make Them Right* (blog). January 22. https://perfectionitself.wordpress.com/2015/01/22/544/.

Eidenmuller, M. E. 2016. American Rhetoric. www.americanrhetoric.com/.

Erway, R. 2010. *Defining "Born Digital."* Online Computer Library Center. Retrieved from www.oclc.org/content/dam/research/activities/hiddencollections/borndigital.pdf.

Flickr. Library of Congress. www.flickr.com/photos/library_of_congress/sets/.

Fried, R. L. 2005. *The Game of School: Why We All Play It, How It Hurts Kids, and What It Will Take to Change It*. Hoboken, NJ: Jossey-Bass.

Gallagher, K. 2011. *Write Like This: Teaching Real-World Writing through Modeling and Mentor Texts*. Portland, ME: Stenhouse Publishers.

Graff, G., and C. Birkenstein. 2009. *"They Say, I Say": The Moves That Matter in Academic Writing.* 2nd ed. New York: W. W. Norton.

Hale, Katharine. 2016. "Branding Student Writing." *TEaCHitivity*, January 27. https://teachitivity. wordpress.com/2016/01/27/branding-student-writing/.

Harris, J. 2006. *Rewriting: How to Do Things with Texts.* Logan, UT: Utah State University Press.

Hicks, T. 2013. *Crafting Digital Writing: Composing Texts Across Media and Genres.* Portsmouth, NH: Heinemann.

Hicks, T., ed. 2015. "Introduction: An Invitation to Look Closely at Students' Work." In *Assessing Students' Digital Writing: Protocols for Looking Closely.* New York: Teachers College Press.

Hicks, T., and D. Perrin. 2014. "Beyond Single Modes and Media: Writing as an Ongoing Multimodal Text Production." In *Handbook of Writing and Text Production*, edited by E. M. Jakobs and D. Perrin. Berlin and New York: Mouton de Gruyter.

Hicks, T., and K. H. Turner. 2013. "No Longer a Luxury: Digital Literacy Can't Wait." *English Journal* 102 (6): 58–65.

Hicks, T., K. H. Turner, and J. Stratton. 2013. "Reimagining a Writer's Process through Digital Storytelling." *LEARNing Landscapes* 6 (2): 167–183.

Hillocks, G. 1995. *Teaching Writing as Reflective Practice.* New York: Teachers College Press.

———. 2006. *Narrative Writing: Learning a New Model for Teaching.* Portsmouth, NH: Heinemann.

———. 2011. *Teaching Argument Writing, Grades 6–12: Supporting Claims with Relevant Evidence and Clear Reasoning.* Portsmouth, NH: Heinemann.

Hobbs, R. 2010. *Copyright Clarity: How Fair Use Supports Digital Learning.* Thousand Oaks, CA: Corwin.

———.2011. *Digital and Media Literacy: Connecting Culture and Classroom.* Thousand Oaks, CA: Corwin.

Howard, R. M. (n.d.). "Issue Brief: Plagiarism." Retrieved March 20, 2016, from www.ncte.org/college/ briefs/plagiarism.

Hunt, B. 2010. *Teaching Blogging Not Blogs.* National Writing Project, October 19. http://digitalis.nwp. org/resource/1198.

Hyler, J., and T. Hicks. 2014. *Create, Compose, Connect! Reading, Writing, and Learning with Digital Tools.* New York: Routledge.

Jiwa, B. 2016. "Brand Story." *The Story of Telling* (blog). http://thestoryoftelling.com/brand-story-services/.

Johnson, A. 2014. "The Ethics of Retweeting and Whether It Amounts to Endorsement." NPR Ombudsman, July 31. www.npr.org/sections/ombudsman/2014/07/31/336921115/the-ethics-of-retweeting-and-whether-it-amounts-to-endorsement.

Journey Staff. 2014. "'It's Beautiful': Coke Debuts Inspiring Ad During Big Game." Coca-Cola Journey, February 14. www.coca-colacompany.com/stories/americaisbeautiful-coke-debuts-inspiring-ad-during-big-game.

Kidd, S. M. 2003. *The Secret Life of Bees.* New York: Penguin Books.

Kohn, A. *Alfie Kohn.* www.alfiekohn.org.

KQED Education. 2016. "About Do Now." ww2.kqed.org/education/about-do-now/.

Lenhart, A., S. Arafeh, A. Smith, and A. R. Macgill. 2008. *Writing, Technology and Teens*. Washington D.C: Pew Internet and American Life Project The College Board's National Commission on Writing. Retrieved from files.eric.ed.gov/fulltext/ED524313.pdf.

Lessig, L. 2009. *Remix: Making Art and Commerce Thrive in the Hybrid Economy*. New York: Penguin Books.

Lunsford, A. A., J. J. Ruszkiewicz, and K. Walters. 2013. *Everything's an Argument*. 6th ed. Boston, MA: Bedford/St. Martins.

MacArthur, D. 1962. "Duty, Honor, Country." Sylvanus Thayer Award Acceptance Address. www.americanrhetoric.com/speeches/douglasmacarthurthayeraward.html.

Mason, T., and S. Klein. 2012. *Ken Burns: On Story*. Retrieved from https://vimeo.com/40972394.

Mazza, E. 2016. "No, the Powerball Jackpot Isn't Enough to Give Everyone $4.3 Million." *Huffington Post*, January 11. www.huffingtonpost.com/entry/powerball-meme-poverty_us_569457a0e4b086bc1cd4fd3f.

McLeod, S. 2015. "Why Would Students Feel Valued at School?" *Dangerously Irrelevant* (blog), February 25. http://dangerouslyirrelevant.org/2015/02/why-would-students-feel-valued-at-school.html.

Media Education Lab. 2012. *Copyright*. Retrieved from: http://mediaeducationlab.com/copyright.

Mikkelson, D. 2016. "Something for Nothing." Snopes.com. www.snopes.com/inboxer/nothing/nothing.asp.

Miller, C. R., and D. Shepherd. 2004. "Blogging as Social Action: A Genre Analysis of the Weblog." *Into the Blogosphere* (blog collection). University of Minnesota Digital Conservancy. http://conservancy.umn.edu/handle/11299/172818.

Minard, C. 1869. "Map of Napoleon's Disastrous Russian Campaign of 1812." *Wikipedia*. https://en.wikipedia.org/wiki/Charles_Joseph_Minard#Work.

Mintz, A. P. 2002. *Web of Deception: Misinformation on the Internet*. Medford, NJ: CyberAge Books.

Moritz, D. 2016. "7 Sup rpowers of a Knockout Infographic: How to Get More Shares and Drive Traffic." *Socially Sorted* (blog). http://sociallysorted.com.au/7-superpowers-of-a-knockout-infographic/.

National Governors Association Center for Best Practices and the Council of Chief State School Officers. 2010. *Common Core State Standards*. ELA-Literacy.W.7.6. Washington, DC: National Governors Association Center for Best Practices and the Council of Chief State School Officers.

National Writing Project, D. DeVoss, E. Eidman-Aadahl, and T. Hicks. 2010. *Because Digital Writing Matters: Improving Student Writing in Online and Multimedia Environments*. San Francisco: Jossey-Bass.

Nielsen Company. 2014. *An Era of Growth: The Cross-Platform Report*. http://www.nielsen.com/us/en/insights/reports/2014/an-era-of-growth-the-cross-platform-report.html.

Palfrey, J., and U. Gasser. 2008. *Born Digital: Understanding the First Generation of Digital Natives*. New York: Basic Books.

Pariser, E. 2011. "Beware Online 'Filter Bubbles.'" TED talk, March. www.ted.com/talks/eli_pariser_beware_online_filter_bubbles?language=en#t-514523.

———. 2012. *The Filter Bubble: How the New Personalized Web Is Changing What We Read and How We Think*. New York: Penguin Books.

PBS NewsHour Extra. 2015. "Has Standardized Testing in the U.S. Gone Too Far?" KQED Education, November 6. ww2.kqed.org/education/2015/11/06/has-standardized-testing-in-the-u-s-gone-too-far/.

Pink, D. 2011. *Drive: The Surprising Truth About What Motivates Us.* New York, NY: Riverhead Books/Penguin.

Raff, J. 2014. "Dear Parents, You Are Being Lied To." *IFL Science* (blog). www.iflscience.com/health-and-medicine/dear-parents-you-are-being-lied.

———. *Violent Metaphors: Thoughts from the Intersection of Science, Pseudoscience, and Conflict* (blog). http://violentmetaphors.com/.

Reed, D., and T. Hicks. 2015. *Research Writing Rewired: Lessons That Ground Students' Digital Learning.* Thousand Oaks, CA: Sage.

Reflection Press (blog). 2013. "Inspiring Change, Changing History," June 24. www.reflectionpress.com/blog/2013/06/24/inspiring-change-changing-history/.

Rheingold, H. 2012. *Net Smart: How to Thrive Online*. Cambridge, MA: MIT Press.

Roy Rosenzweig Center for History and New Media at George Mason University. 2016. "Zotero." www.zotero.org/.

Schneider, Steven. 2016. "People Obviously Aren't Doing the Math on This Facebook Meme About the $1.3 Billion Powerball Jackpot." *Tech Times*, January 11. www.techtimes.com/articles/123577/20160111/people-obviously-arent-doing-math-facebook-meme-1-3-billion.htm.

Schwartz, K. 2013. "How to Help Kids Find Their Aspirations." *Mindshift*, October 3. http://ww2.kqed.org/mindshift/2013/10/03/how-to-help-kids-find-their-aspirations/

Schwartz, T., and C. Porath. 2014. "The Power of Meeting Your Employees' Needs." *Harvard Business Review*, June 30. https://hbr.org/2014/06/the-power-of-meeting-your-employees-needs.

Selber, S. 2004. *Multiliteracies for a Digital Age*. Carbondale, IL: Southern Illinois University Press.

Selfe, C. L., and G. E. Hawisher. 2004. *Literate Lives in the Information Age: Narratives of Literacy from the United States*. New York: Routledge.

Silverman, C. ed. 2016. *The Verification Handbook: A Definitive Guide to Verifying Digital Content for Emergency Coverage*. http://verificationhandbook.com/.

Smith, M., D. Appleman, and J. D. Wilhelm. 2014. *Uncommon Core: Where the Authors of the Standards Go Wrong About Instruction—and How You Can Get It Right*. Thousand Oaks, CA: Corwin.

Smith, M., and J. D. Wilhelm. 2006. *Going with the Flow: How to Engage Boys (and Girls) in Their Literacy Learning*. Portsmouth, NH: Heinemann.

Smith, M., J. D. Wilhelm, and J. E. Fredricksen. 2012. *Oh, Yeah?!: Putting Argument to Work Both in School and Out*. Portsmouth, NH: Heinemann.

Sobol, D. J. 1967. *Two-Minute Mysteries.* New York: Scholastic.

Strals, N., and B. Willen. 2015. "Which 2016 Presidential Candidate Has the Worst Logo?" *Washington Post*, July 31. www.washingtonpost.com/posteverything/wp/2015/07/31/which-2016-presidential-candidate-has-the-worst-logo/.

Strong, W. 2006. *Write for Insight: Empowering Content Area Learning, Grades 6–12*. Boston, MA: Pearson.

Sullivan, L. 2013. (aka Barrett.Discovery) DSC06585, November 25. https://www.flickr.com/photos/projectdiscovery/12373788014/sizes/s/.

Teeman, T. October 13, 2013. "Why Millions Love Elise Andrew's Science Page." *The Guardian*, www.theguardian.com/science/2013/oct/13/i-fucking-love-science-elsie-andrew.

Thompson, C. 2010. "Clive Thompson on How Tweets and Texts Nurture In-Depth Analysis." *Wired*, December 27. www.wired.com/2010/12/st_thompson_short_long/.

Toulmin, S. E. 1958/2003. *The Uses of Argument*. New York: Cambridge University Press.

Toulmin, S., R. D. Rieke, and A. Janik. 1979. *An Introduction to Reasoning*. New York: MacMillan.

Treat, L. 1981. *Crime and Puzzlement*. Boston, MA: Godine.

———. 1983. *You're the Detective*. Boston, MA: Godine.

Tufte, E. 1983. *The Visual Display of Quantitative Information*. 2nd ed. Cheshire, CT: Graphics Press.

Turner, K. H. 2005. "Toulmin and Transfer: The Impact of Instruction in Argument on Students' Writing Across Disciplines." (Ph.D. diss., Rutgers University). http://search.proquest.com/docview/305429989/1402803DD8F6ED5256E/3?accountid=10181.

Turner, K. H., and T. Hicks. 2015. *Connected Reading: Teaching Adolescent Readers in a Digital World*. Urbana, IL: National Council of Teachers of English.

Turner, K. H., and T. Hicks. 2015. "Connected Reading is the Heart of Research." *English Journal,* 105, 41–48.

Valenza, J. 2016. "Copyright-Friendly and Copyleft." https://copyrightfriendly.wikispaces.com/.

Vicario, M. D., et al. 2016. "The Spreading of Misinformation Online." *Proceedings of the National Academy of Sciences* 113 (3): 554–559.

Vis, F. 2014. "To Tackle the Spread of Misinformation Online We Must First Understand It." *The Guardian*, April 24. www.theguardian.com/commentisfree/2014/apr/24/tackle-spread-misinformation-online.

West, R., Pineau, J., and Precup, D. 2009. "Wikispeedia: An Online Game for Inferring Semantic Distances Between Concepts." In *Proceedings of the 21st International Joint Conference on Artificial Intelligence* (pp. 1598–1603). San Francisco: Morgan Kaufmann Publishers. Retrieved from http://dl.acm.org/citation.cfm?id=1661445.1661702.

Wiggins, G., and J. McTighe. 2005. *Understanding by Design*. 2nd ed. Alexandria, VA: Association for Supervision and Curriculum Development.

Wikipedia. s.v. "Blog." https://en.wikipedia.org/wiki/Blog.

Wikipedia. s.v. "Infographic." https://en.wikipedia.org/wiki/Infographic.

Wikipedia. s.v. "Internet Meme." https://en.wikipedia.org/wiki/Internet_meme.

Wikipedia. s.v. "Wiki-Link Game." https://en.wikipedia.org/wiki/Wikipedia:Wiki-Link_Game.

Wikispeedia. http://cs.mcgill.ca/~rwest/wikispeedia/project.php.

Williams, R. 2014. *The Non-designer's Design Book: Design and Typographic Principles for the Visual Novice.* 4th ed. Berkeley, CA: Peachpit Press.

Wise, R., producer and director. 1965. *The Sound of Music* (motion picture). Robert Wise Productions.

WNYC Studios. n.d. "Breaking News Consumer's Handbook." *On the Media.* www.wnyc.org/series/breaking-news-consumers-handbook/ and www.wnyc.org/story/breaking-news-consumers-handbook-pdf/.

WNYC Studios. *On the Media.* www.wnyc.org/shows/otm/.

World Economic Forum. 2013. "Digital Wildfires in a Hyperconnected World." *Global Risks Report 2013.* http://reports.weforum.org/global-risks-2013/risk-case-1/digital-wildfires-in-a-hyperconnected-world/.

———. 2014. "10. The Rapid Spread of Misinformation Online." Retrieved February 29, 2016, from http://reports.weforum.org/outlook-14/top-ten-trends-category-page/10-the-rapid-spread-of-misinformation-online/.

Writing in Digital Environments Research Center Collective. 2005. "Why Teach Digital Writing?" http://english.ttu.edu/kairos/10.1/binder2.html?coverweb/wide/index.html.

Youth Radio/KQED Education. 2016. "What Does Being Politically Active Mean to You?" *Do Now News and Civics* (blog), January 14. https://youthradio.org/journalism/education/what-does-being-politically-active-mean-to-you/.

Programs/Websites Mentioned

Chapter 1
- IFL Science: www.iflscience.com/
- Violent metaphors: https://violentmetaphors.com/

Chapter 2
- Amazon: www.amazon.com/
- Mematic: www.mematic.net/
- Yelp: www.yelp.com/

Chapter 3
- Copyright Confusion: http://copyrightconfusion.wikispaces.com/Reasoning/
- Dangerously Irrelevant: http://dangerouslyirrelevant.org/
- Feedly: www.feedly.com/
- Feedspot: www.feedspot.com/
- Media Education Lab: http://mediaeducationlab.com/copyright/
- Perfection Itself blog: https://perfectionitself.wordpress.com/

Chapter 4
- Centers for Disease Control and Prevention: www.cdc.gov/
- Citelighter: www.citelighter.com/
- Diigo: www.diigo.com/
- Easel.ly: www.easel.ly/
- EasyBib: www.easybib.com/
- EndNote basic: http://endnote.com/product-details/basic
- Evernote: https://evernote.com/
- Food Republic: www.foodrepublic.com/
- Google Keep: https://play.google.com/store/apps/details?id=com.google.android.keep&hl=en
- Infogr.am: https://infogr.am/
- JustStand.org: www.juststand.org/
- Learnist: (application)
- *New York Times Well* blog: http://well.blogs.nytimes.com/
- No Kid Hungry: www.nokidhungry.org/
- OneNote: www.onenote.com/
- Pew Research Center: www.pewresearch.org/
- Piktochart: http://piktochart.com/
- Pinterest: www.pinterest.com/

- RefME: www.refme.com/us/
- Scoop.It!: www.scoop.it/
- U.S. Census Bureau: www.census.gov/
- U.S. Department of Education: www.ed.gov/

Chapter 5

- Alfie Kohn: www.alfiekohn.org/
- American Eagle Outfitters: www.ae.com/
- Animoto: https://animoto.com/
- Audacity: www.audacityteam.org/
- Central Intelligence Agency: www.cia.gov/index.html
- Creative Commons: https://creativecommons.org/
- EDpuzzle: www.edpuzzle.org/
- iMovie: www.apple.com/mac/imovie/
- Internet Archive: https://archive.org/index.php
- Jing: www.techsmith.com/jing.html
- Mind Over Media: http://propaganda.mediaeducationlab.com/
- NASA: www.nasa.gov/
- National Parks Service: www.nps.gov/index.htm
- PlayPosit: www.playposit.com/
- Ponder: www.ponder.co/welcome/
- Screencastify: www.screencastify.com/
- Screencast-O-Matic: https://screencast-o-matic.com/home
- Seventeen: www.seventeen.com/
- Vialogues: https://vialogues.com/
- VoicetThread: https://voicethread.com/
- WeVideo: www.wevideo.com/
- Wikimedia Commons: https://commons.wikimedia.org/wiki/Main_Page
- Windows Movie Maker: http://support.microsoft.com/en-us/help/14220/windows-movie-maker-download

Chapter 6

- ABC News: http://abcnews.go.com/
- CNET: www.cnet.com/
- DomainTools Whois: https://whois.domaintools.com/
- Facebook: www.facebook.com
- FactCheck.org: www.factcheck.org/
- Google: www.google.com

- Hackpad: https://hackpad.com/
- *Huffington Post*: www.huffingtonpost.com/
- Instagram: www.instagram.com/
- *New York Times Room for Debate* blog: www.nytimes.com/roomfordebate
- Pew Research Center: www.pewresearch.org/
- PolitiFact: www.politifact.com/
- ProCon.org: www.procon.org/
- ProPublica: www.propublica.org/
- Reflection Press: www.reflectionpress.com/
- Snagit: www.techsmith.com/snagit.html
- Snopes: www.snopes.com/
- Tumblr: www.tumblr.com
- Twitter: http://twitter.com
- Vine: https://vine.co/
- Wayback Machine: https://archive.org/web/
- *Wikipedia*: www.wikipedia.org/

Chapter 7

- Amazon: www.amazon.com/
- Awesome Screenshot: www.awesomescreenshot.com/
- Camtasia: www.techsmith.com/camtasia.html
- Educreations: www.educreations.com/
- Explain Everything: http://explaineverything.com/
- FireShot: http://getfireshot.com/
- Genius: http://genius.com/
- Hypothes.is: https://hypothes.is/
- Jing: www.techsmith.com/jing.html
- Monosnap: www.monosnap.com/welcome
- Preview: https://support.apple.com/en-us/HT201740
- QuickTime: https://support.apple.com/downloads/quicktime
- Screencastify: www.screencastify.com/
- Screencast-O-Matic: https://screencast-o-matic.com/
- ShowMe: www.showme.com/
- Yelp: www.yelp.com/nyc

Index